MEN *of*
CHARACTER

Nehemiah

Becoming
a Disciplined
Leader

GENE A. GETZ

Foreword by Dr. Bruce H. Wilkinson

BROADMAN
&HOLMAN
PUBLISHERS

Nashville, Tennessee

D0179512

Printed in the United States of America

Published by:
Broadman & Holman Publishers
Nashville, Tennessee

Design: Steven Boyd

4261-65
0-8054-6165-5

Dewey Decimal Classification: 248.842
Subject Heading: Men \ Nehemiah \ Christian Life
Library of Congress Card Catalog Number: 94-40764

Unless otherwise noted, Scriptures are from the New American
Standard Bible, © the Lockman Foundation, 1960, 1962, 1963,
1968, 1971, 1972, 1973, 1975, 1977; used by permission. Other
versions used are NIV, the Holy Bible, New International Version,
copyright © 1973, 1978, 1984 by International Bible Society; KJV,
King James Version; and RSV, Revised Standard Version of the Bible,
copyrighted 1946, 1952, © 1971, 1973.

Library of Congress Cataloging-in-Publication Data
Getz, Gene A.
    Nehemiah : becoming a disciplined leader / Gene Getz.
        p. cm. — (Men of character)
        Rev. ed.
        Includes bibliographical references.
        ISBN 0-8054-6165-5
        1. Nehemiah (biblical figure). 2. Bible. O.T. Nehemiah—
Criticism, interpretation, etc. I. Title. II. Series: Getz, Gene A.
    Men of character.
    BS580.J7G471995
    222'.2092—dc20
    94-40764
    CIP
        3 4 5 99

I want to dedicate this book to my good friend and colleague, Bruce Wilkinson, founder and president of Walk Thru The Bible Ministries. I remember first meeting Bruce as one of my students at Dallas Theological Seminary. During our initial conversation, I sensed that he had great leadership potential. He, of course, has proved that over the years in giving birth to Walk Thru The Bible Ministries and leading this great organization that has touched lives literally around the world. In addition, Bruce also leads the CoMission—a movement of nearly one hundred Christian organizations who have joined together in unprecedented unity to send thousands of Christians to serve the Lord in the former Soviet Union.

It's a privilege to dedicate this book to Bruce—a man who exemplifies in unusual ways the principles that emerge from Nehemiah's role as a dynamic leader in Israel.

Other books in the *Men of Character* series:
Elijah: Remaining Steadfast through Uncertainty
Joshua: Living as a Consistent Role Model
Jacob: Following God without Looking Back
Moses: Freeing Yourself to Know God
Joseph: Overcoming Obstacles through Faithfulness
Abraham: Holding Fast to the Will of God
David: Seeking God Faithfully
Samuel: A Lifetime Serving God
Daniel: Standing Firm for God
The Apostles: Becoming Unified through Diversity

Contents

Foreword by Bruce H. Wilkinson ix

Introduction: An Amazing Man! 1

1. A Powerful Prayer Process 3

2. Walking the Tight Rope 20

3. God's Hands—Our Hands 36

4. A Great Leadership Model 49

5. Overcoming Discouragement 65

6. Handling a Conspiracy 81

7. An Incredible Fifty-two Days 96

8. Conflict Resolution 112

9. Promotion with a Proper Perspective 127

10. When People Try to Hurt You 144

11. A Water Gate Experience 161

12. A Leader's Toughest Task 176

Notes 194

Foreword

*M*eet one of the greatest leaders of all time. His name is Nehemiah. And my good friend, Gene Getz, brings him to life in this Old Testament study.

Whether you're a leader in your home, your church, or in your business, Nehemiah will teach you leadership principles that will work in every situation.

If you face discouragement, in yourself and others, he'll teach you how to face it and emerge victorious.

If morale has dropped out of sight, he'll teach you how to get people out of the cellar and out where they can once again see the "sunshine."

If you struggle with conflict among your people, he'll teach you how to resolve it God's way.

You name it, Nehemiah faced it! But every time—with the "help of his God"—he succeeded, even against impossible odds.

One of the greatest things Nehemiah will teach you is how to pray. Dr. Getz shares how he personally used the "Nehemiah Prayer Process" in his own church planting ministry and experienced incredible and miraculous answers to prayer.

I first met Gene Getz when I was a student at Dallas Theological Seminary. I was fresh out of Bible college, and before long, Gene became one of my favorite and most stimulating professors. And as the years went by, he became a friend, then a mentor, and also one of my thesis advisors. My topic was "Walk Thru The Bible."

As you can see, God has used Gene to strategically mark my life and ministry. In the classroom, I discovered he was a master at applying the Scriptures to the needs of contemporary culture. In the church, I discovered he was a sensitive pastor who modeled servant-leadership that attracted and blossomed his congregation to their fullest potential for the Lord. And in his private life as a man of God, I soon found myself admiring and respecting his life of focus and discipline.

Perhaps that's why I'm so thrilled Gene has written on this strategic subject of leadership—he models it with excellence!

I'm thankful Gene has given us another insightful book. You'll enjoy it, you'll learn from it, and I'm confident you'll become a better leader! The practical, goal-setting opportunities at the end of each chapter can change your life. This book will help you "plan your work" and "work your plan!"

Dr. Bruce H. Wilkinson
President, Walk Thru The Bible Ministries
Chairman, The CoMission

An Amazing Man!

*N*ehemiah was truly one of the great leaders of all time. The principles that flow from his life to ours are profound, powerful, and practical!

Nehemiah's experience touches all of us—whether we are husband, father, pastor, CEO, president, supervisor, or director. He models:

➤ how to pray when there seems to be no human solution to our problems;

➤ how to blend human and divine factors when facing incredible predicaments;

➤ how to keep God's sovereign control of the universe and our human responsibility in proper balance;

➤ how to "plan our work" and "work our plan"—and, at the same time, rely on God as our divine resource Person;

➤ how to handle discouragement in ourselves and others;

➤ how to set goals and achieve them when everything around us seems to be falling apart;

➤ how to motivate others when morale is at an all-time low;

➤ how to cope with anger and other negative emotions;

➤ how to accept promotion and success without abusing or misusing our privileges;

➤ how to respond to those who make false accusations against us and malign our motives;

➤ how to help others develop God's perspective on life;

➤ how to face and solve some of the toughest problems we'll ever face.

Nehemiah truly was an amazing man! Let his life touch yours. Though most of us will never have to face challenges to the same degree as this Old Testament personality, we will, at some time, experience the same struggles. Even "little problems" seem big when they touch our emotions. And Nehemiah's perspective on prayer and persistence will help all of us to face life's challenges and emerge victorious. Indeed, Nehemiah teaches us that we "can do all things through Him who strengthens [us]" (Phil. 4:13).

Welcome to another exciting Old Testament character study!

Chapter 1

A Powerful Prayer Process
Read Nehemiah 1:1–11

*N*ehemiah's life and example means a great deal to me personally. His approach to prayer—when faced with what appeared to be an impossible task—has marked my own life! I've often used his "prayer process" as a model when I've faced difficult challenges in my own ministry.

Later, I'll share some of the most miraculous answers to prayer I've ever experienced. As you'll see, it wasn't just coincidental that these answers resulted when a group of us followed Nehemiah's "prayer process."

A Man God Used

There are some individuals who have a *special* place in God's scheme of things—people God chooses to use in unique ways to achieve His purposes. Nehemiah is one of those special people.

Though his life story does not occupy the same amount of space as some of the other Old Testament leaders God chose to impact the children of Israel, Nehemiah certainly stands tall on the pages of Scripture as a dynamic spiritual leader. In fact, we can learn more about this man's specific leadership qualities and skills than most Bible characters.

Nehemiah was apparently born during the exile period. His father's name was Hacaliah (see 1:1), and his grandparents were probably taken into captivity when Jerusalem fell to the Babylonians. Beyond this, we really know very little about his family background. He suddenly appears as an adult standing ready to be used to achieve God's purposes.

Sin Divides

Because of King Solomon's sins, the kingdom of Israel split into two parts. The northern tribes were ruled initially by Jeroboam and the southern tribes (Judah and Benjamin) were ruled by Rehoboam. Both kingdoms continued to be characterized by idolatry and immorality. And as God had forewarned, He judged *all* Israel. The northern tribes were taken into captivity by the Assyrians. Years later, those in the Southern Kingdom were deported by the Babylonians.

The children of Israel who made up the Northern Kingdom were absorbed into the various cultures and communities of the world. However, the people of the Southern Kingdom remained intact. When the Medes and Persians captured Babylon, many of the children of Israel began to return to the land of Canaan. This happened approximately seventy years after their deportation (see fig. 1-1).

Figure 1-1

Rebuilding the Temple

The first group returned to Judah under the leadership of Zerubabel in approximately 536 B.C. In spite of tremendous opposition from the Samaritans, they eventually succeeded in rebuilding the temple (see fig. 1-2).

Panorama of Ezra-Nehemiah

Return Under Zerubbabel	The Influence of Esther (484–465 B.C.)	Return Under Ezra	Return of Nehemiah
Rebuilding the Temple		Spiritual Reform	Constructing the Walls of Jerusalem
Ezra 1–6	Esther	Ezra 7–10	Nehemiah 1–13
536	516	458	444 425

Figure 1-2

Renewal in Israel

Ezra led a second group of Jews back to the promised land (see Ezra 7:1–10) nearly a century later. When they arrived, they discovered that those that had gone on before them and the children that were born during this time were in a state of spiritual and moral deterioration. Like their forefathers, they had intermarried with the unbelieving people in the surrounding nations and were engaging in horrible idolatry and other pagan practices.

Ezra faced the problem head-on and began to teach God's laws. As usually happened, when God's people are faithfully taught His will, they began to turn from their sins.

Rebuilding the Walls

Ezra's ministry set the stage for Nehemiah's appearance in Israel. Under difficult conditions, he challenged the children of Israel to rebuild the walls of the city and eventually led them to reorder their spiritual, social, and economic life—a miraculous accomplishment.

A Powerful Model!

One of the major goals of this book is to look carefully at Nehemiah's leadership style. His example provides a powerful model for all of us—no matter what our position in life. Whether husband, father, manager, executive, Sunday School superintendent, youth leader, or pastor—we'll learn principles that will help all of us function more productively as members of God's eternal family. His journal—the book that bears his name—is alive with lessons that can change our lives and those we lead.

A Man of Character

Sometime after the Jews began to return to Canaan, Nehemiah caught the eye of King Artaxerxes, the king of Persia. He became this mighty monarch's personal cupbearer—the man who tasted his wine and guarded his sleeping quarters. King Artaxerxes no doubt also consulted him for advice and wisdom.

The very fact that Nehemiah occupied this role in the king's court demonstrates his sterling character. This pagan king would never trust a man who had not exemplified total honesty, trustworthiness, and outstanding wisdom. As we'll soon see, Nehemiah was this kind of man because he never forsook the God of Abraham, Isaac, and Jacob. He had a great love for the Lord and committed himself to keeping the laws of God in spite of his pagan environment.

A Man of Compassion

In the midst of his life of luxury, Nehemiah's routine was interrupted one day by a group of men who had come from

Judah. One of them was his brother Hanani. You can imagine Nehemiah's excitement! This was his first opportunity to visit a close family member who had returned to Jerusalem. It was also his first opportunity to get information about the Jews who had left earlier under the leadership of Zerubabel and Ezra. But the joy he may have experienced initially suddenly turned sour. The report was grim: "The remnant there in the province who survived the captivity are in great distress and reproach, and the wall of Jerusalem is broken down and its gates are burned with fire" (Neh. 1:3).

Nehemiah was so distressed and emotionally distraught over this bad news that he "sat down and wept and mourned for days" (v. 4). We're not told exactly how long this went on, but some estimate that it could have been at least four months. He was so focused on the plight of his fellow Jews that he refused to eat—at least on a regular basis—and devoted hours and days to prayer (see v. 4).

Think for a moment what this means! Nehemiah had access to the king's kitchen and the most exquisite food and drink in the land. How easy it would have been to avoid the Jerusalem problem! Rather than fasting, he could have "eaten away" his anxiety and "drowned his sorrows" with food and drink. But he didn't! He couldn't—or wouldn't—allow himself to escape the emotional pain. His own comfortable existence only accentuated his concern for his brothers and sisters who had returned to Jerusalem.

All of these attitudes and actions give evidence of Nehemiah's honorable character—and his deep concern for others. Unselfishness is, of course, a very powerful character trait.

A Man of Prayer

It's not an accident that the Holy Spirit led Nehemiah to describe his prayer experience. He not only outlined *how* he prayed but *what* he prayed.

He Acknowledged God's Greatness

Nehemiah faced a predicament he knew he could not resolve by himself. From a purely human point of view, it was an impossible situation. But Nehemiah also knew that God is not restricted by human limitations. He is the omnipotent God. With Him all things are possible because of who He is! This was Nehemiah's view of God, which explains why he begins his prayer "I beseech Thee, O Lord [Yahweh] God of heaven, the *great* and *awesome* God. . . . "(v. 5).*

In the midst of his own despair, Nehemiah lifted his heart upward and acknowledged God's unfathomable greatness— His incomparable power, His omniscience, His omnipresence, and His majesty. By using the divine name Yahweh, Nehemiah was also acknowledging that God never reneges on His promises. This explains what he said next in his prayer.

He Reminded God of His Covenant with Israel

"I beseech Thee, O Lord [Yahweh] God of heaven . . . who *preserves the covenant* and lovingkindnesses for those who love Him and keep His commandments" (v. 5). Later in his prayer, Nehemiah became even more specific in reminding God of His promises to Israel:

> "Remember the word which Thou didst command Thy servant Moses, saying, 'If you are unfaithful I will scatter you among the peoples; but if you return to Me and keep My commandments and do them, though those of you who have been scattered were in the most remote part of the heavens, I will gather them from there and will bring them to the place where I have chosen to cause My name to dwell.'" (vv. 8–9)

Why did Nehemiah remind an omniscient God of His promises? If He is all-knowing, how could He forget?

Of course God never forgets! However, this is a powerful lesson we can learn about prayer. It pleases the Lord to hear His children reiterate His promises when they're talking with Him.

*Author uses italics for emphasis in Scripture.

In Nehemiah's case, it indicates something else. Not all of the children of Israel had forsaken the Lord. Nehemiah was one of them. On the other hand, like his predecessor Daniel (see Dan. 9:4–6), Nehemiah included himself in Israel's sins.

He Confessed Israel's Sin

"Let Thine ear be attentive and Thine eyes opened to hear the prayer of Thy servant which I am praying before Thee now, day and night, on behalf of the sons of Israel Thy servants, confessing the sins of the sons of Israel which we have sinned against Thee; *I and my Father's house have sinned. We have acted very corruptly against Thee* and have not kept the commandments, nor the statutes, nor the ordinances which Thou didst command Thy servant Moses" (Neh. 1:6–7).

Nehemiah and Daniel both remained true to God during the captivity. However, they didn't rationalize away their involvement in Israel's corporate failure as a nation. This is why they confessed Israel's sin—and included themselves.

But Nehemiah and Daniel were not the only ones who had remained true to God during the captivity. This is also apparent from Nehemiah's prayer. There were others who hadn't bowed down to false gods. Thus he prayed: "O Lord, I beseech Thee, may Thine ear be attentive to *the prayer of Thy servant* and *the prayer of Thy servants* who delight to revere Thy name" (v. 11).

Throughout the history of Israel, no matter how serious their sins and in spite of their failure as a nation, there was always a remnant who refused to follow paganism. Like Daniel's three friends—Shadrach, Meshach, and Abednego—they often stood alone, refusing to serve any god but the One who brought them out of the land of Egypt and into Canaan (see Dan. 3:12). While many paid the ultimate price by giving their lives, there were others whom God protected. Nehemiah was one—which I'm sure added to his sense of obligation to do something for his extended family in Jerusalem. Like Esther, he sensed he had attained his royal position "for such a time as this" (Esther 4:14).

He Asked God for Specific Help

During the prolonged period when Nehemiah prayed and fasted, God apparently made it clear to him that there was only one individual on earth who could help him encourage his fellow Jews in Jerusalem—it was the king he served. This is why Nehemiah prayed so specifically, "Make Thy servant successful today, and grant him compassion before *this man*" (v. 11b). "The man" he was referring to was King Artaxerxes.

An Unselfish Man!

Nehemiah's specific prayer request also reflects his character. He was not only willing to pray for his people, but he was also willing to be the channel through whom God could work to deliver His people out of their desperate situation in Jerusalem.

This was certainly not a simple decision for Nehemiah. He was not naive. He knew what lay ahead of him. To leave the king's court and go to Jerusalem would mean giving up his choice position that provided him with incredible security and safety. It would mean risking his life—which Nehemiah was willing to do!

This is the ultimate demonstration of love and unselfishness. This is what Jesus Christ did centuries later, and the apostle John reminds us that this is how we know what love really is! Jesus Christ "laid down His life for us; and we ought to lay down our lives for the brethren" (1 John 3:16). Nehemiah was this kind of man long before he had Jesus Christ's incomparable example.

Becoming God's Man Today

Principles to Live By

If you've been open to the leadership of the Holy Spirit in your own life, you've probably already noticed some convicting lessons that have grown out of our study. Nehemiah's personal integrity, his deep concern, his unselfishness, and his intense compassion and love for others jump off the pages of Scripture.

But what about his prayer life? Nehemiah definitely believed that "the effective prayer of a righteous man can accomplish much" (James 5:16). This wasn't something that he simply talked about. He prayed! In the midst of this time of crisis, he poured out his heart and soul to God.

Nehemiah demonstrates that in our moments of pain and helplessness we need to remember that we have access to God— the One who can help us make our way through life's greatest moments of darkness. Nehemiah fleshes out the words of David when he wrote, "Even though I walk through the valley of the shadow of death, I fear no evil; for Thou art with me" (Ps. 23:4).

What makes Nehemiah's prayer so unique is that he outlines for us a process that we can apply to our own lives during periods of crisis. Before we look at the specific steps in this process and how they apply to our lives, we need to look at his attitudes and actions prior to the prayer itself. This is as much a part of what happened as the very words that flowed from his lips.

Principle 1. Like Nehemiah, we must pray out of a heart of deep concern.

Nehemiah's heart was deeply moved with compassion for the suffering Jews in Jerusalem, so much so that he persisted in his prayer day after day. Consequently, God's own heart was touched.

A Parable from Jesus

Jesus taught us this truth with the parable of the unrighteous judge and the poor widow. The judge whom Jesus referred to was a man who did "not fear God" or "respect man" (Luke 18:4). However, he responded to the woman's request for help. This was primarily because she kept bothering him.

If a pagan magistrate would listen to a poor widow, how much more will God—who is a *righteous judge*—"bring about justice for His elect, who cry to Him day and night" (Luke 18:7). Nehemiah is an Old Testament illustration of the truth Jesus was teaching that day.

Principle 2. Like Nehemiah, we must make prayer a priority over other needs.

Fasting is often associated with prayer. For example, consider the men who were meeting together in the church in Antioch. Paul and Barnabas were among them and it was during this period—"while they were ministering to the Lord *and fasting*"—that the Holy Spirit said, "Set apart for Me Barnabas and Saul for the work to which I have called them" (Acts 13:1–2).

The purpose for fasting is not to abstain from food per se in order to experience God's special grace. Rather, fasting demonstrates to God that we are willing to spend time talking to Him rather than meeting our physical needs.

Another Illustration

The apostle Paul referred to abstaining from sexual relations in marriage on occasions in order to spend time in prayer. In fact, he made it very clear that this was the *only* reason to abstain from this marital responsibility (see 1 Cor. 7:5).

In both of these examples, the Scriptures are teaching us that there are times when we should abstain from meeting our physical and emotional needs in order to spend time communicating with God about concerns and needs that are more important. And when we do this, God's heart is touched in a special way. It demonstrates our sincerity and our willingness to sacrifice our own needs and desires so as to get His attention. It's a true test of our motives—and what is most important in our lives.

Nehemiah illustrates all of this in a powerful way. Though he had access to the best food in the kingdom, he refrained from eating so that he could devote his time to prayer. Day after day and week after week he poured out his soul before the Lord for his brothers and sisters in Jerusalem. Consequently, God's heart was deeply moved.

Principle 3. Like Nehemiah, we must pray persistently.

Jesus confirmed this principle in the previous parable. The unrighteous judge responded to the poor widow because "she *kept coming* to him" with her request (Luke 18:3).

Again, the point is clear! If a wealthy man of the world who could care less about the deep needs of a poor woman responded to her persistence, how much more will God— who cares about our every need—respond when we "cry to Him day and night" (Luke 18:7; cf. Matt. 6:25–26).

Nehemiah certainly illustrates this truth works. God honored his persistent prayers!

Principle 4. Like Nehemiah, we must recognize tha. God is great and awesome.

Since God is an absolutely holy God and the sovereign Lord of the universe, we must approach Him with reverence and awe. Jesus also taught His disciples this truth with His own model prayer when He said, "Pray, then, in this way: 'Our Father who art in heaven, *hallowed be Thy name*'" (Matt. 6:9).

Don't misunderstand! God is also our friend—but we must never take this friendship for granted. He is still God and we are His creation. It's only because of what Jesus Christ has done for us that we can approach His throne of grace.

A New and Living Way

Though God *is* great and awesome, we should not hesitate to approach Him in prayer. We're welcome in His presence every moment of every day. And what is more amazing, He's interested in every detail of our lives. And, He's provided a way to approach Him.

If you have difficulty grasping these great truths, meditate on the following New Testament passage:

Since, therefore, brethren we have confidence to enter the holy place by the blood of Jesus, by a new and living way which He inaugurated for us through the veil, that is, His flesh, and since we have a great high priest over the house of God, let us draw near with a sincere heart and full assurance of faith, having our hearts sprinkled clean from an evil conscience and our bodies washed with pure water. (Heb. 10:19–22)

Principle 5. Like Nehemiah, we should also remind God of His promises to us.

When we verbalize to God what He has promised us, we are demonstrating to Him that we actually *know* what He has said, and we *believe* it.

Think for a moment about a teacher who gives an examination to a group of students. What happens to that teacher emotionally when those students are able to verbalize accurately what they have learned? Having been a teacher for years, I can respond to that question. I feel loved, appreciated—and listened to!

In our humanness, it's difficult for us to understand that God enjoys and appreciates being heard. He responds positively to us when we reiterate in prayer the things that He has taught us. We should never hesitate to remind God of what He already knows!

Principle 6. Like Nehemiah, we must acknowledge our unworthiness and sinfulness, our human weaknesses and failings.

In actuality, we have a unique advantage over Nehemiah. Jesus Christ has died for us, and the apostle John reminds us that "if we walk in the light as He Himself is in the light, we have fellowship with one another, and the blood of Jesus His Son cleanses us from all sin" (1 John 1:7). John also states that "if we confess our sins, He is faithful and righteous to forgive us our sins and to cleanse us from all unrighteousness" (1:9).

What Is Our Advantage?

Nehemiah had to depend on animal sacrifices and the blood of bulls and goats—sacrifices that foreshadowed the perfect Lamb of God (see Heb. 9:11–14). Once Jesus died for us, His blood *keeps on cleansing* us from all sin. We are already forgiven in Christ if we have truly accepted His personal sacrifice for us. However, we must continually walk in the light, acknowledging our sinfulness. As we do, God responds to our prayers.

What Does This Mean?

Does this mean that we should not seek forgiveness when we sin? Not at all! It *does* mean, however, that our salvation is secure in Christ because of the continual cleansing blood of Christ. However, we must walk in fellowship with the Lord, free from deliberate sins if God is going to respond to our prayers. When we knowingly sin against God, we should ask for forgiveness, knowing He has already granted it!

Principle 7. Like Nehemiah, we must be specific in our prayers if we want to get specific answers.

Paul addressed this issue when he wrote to the Philippians: "Be anxious for nothing, but in *everything* by prayer and supplication with thanksgiving let your requests be made known to God" (Phil. 4:6).

Everything that touches our lives is important to God. There is nothing in our lives so small that God is not interested in it. And there is nothing so big that He cannot help us with it. But to get specific answers to prayer, we must be specific in our requests.

When contemplating prayer, meditate on Paul's wonderful conclusion following his specific prayer for the Ephesian Christians: "Now to Him who is able to do exceeding abundantly beyond all that we ask or think, according to the power that works within us, to Him be the glory in the church and in Christ Jesus to all generations forever and ever. Amen" (Eph. 3:19–20).

Practicing Nehemiah's Prayer Process

At the beginning of this chapter, I mentioned that Nehemiah's life and example means a great deal to me personally. The reason relates to his model prayer. Let me illustrate!

I've been involved in church planting since 1972. After starting a church that became very successful, I left the home base to help start a sister church in the Park Cities area of Dallas. A group of us felt confident that God wanted a new witness in this part of the city. We soon discovered, however, that we were faced with what seemed to be an impossible task. Property values were out of sight. The property that was available was scarce and included small plots that were not large enough for a church. The depth of the problem is reflected in the fact that no one had constructed a church building in this part of Dallas for nearly twenty-five years.

We looked and prayed for months—in the meantime meeting on Sunday evenings in a rented facility. To be perfectly honest, many of us were getting very discouraged. We felt we might need to give up and go back to the home-base church. We'd already learned from other experiences in starting several other sister churches that it was very difficult to maintain a ministry in our culture without a permanent facility—particularly in this area of the country.

While I was trying to come to grips with reality, the Holy Spirit directed me to Nehemiah's prayer process. I can remember vividly how I identified with Nehemiah's helpless feelings. From a human point of view, I saw no solution. I also began to wonder how long our small group of people would be willing to participate in a ministry that seemed to be faltering because of our rather dead-end search for property. We were *all* getting restless. Furthermore, even if we "found" some property, how could we pay for it?

The more I studied what Nehemiah did—and how he did it—the more convinced I became that I should share his prayer process with our little church body. As I reflect back, I now know that the Lord gave me faith at that moment in my life to believe that Nehemiah's approach to prayer would also work for us. Consequently, I outlined Nehemiah's experience—just as I've done in the earlier part of this chapter. I then led the church body through the same steps taken by this Old Testament leader. The difference, of course, is that it wasn't just my personal prayers but our prayers together as a group of believers.

1. We acknowledged God's greatness with the use of Scripture, hymns, and prayers. As we worshiped the Lord in this way, we let Him know that we knew and believed that He could find us a piece of property and/or a permanent facility—even though it seemed to be a human impossibility. If He could resolve Nehemiah's predicament, we told the Lord that we believed He could solve ours.

2. We reminded God of His promises to us. I asked various members of the body to openly share scriptural statements with the Lord. Vividly, I remember that one person shared Jesus' own words that are recorded by Matthew in his Gospel—"Ask, and it shall be given to you; seek, and you shall find; knock, and it shall be opened to you. For everyone who asks receives, and he who seeks finds, and to him who knocks it shall be opened" (Matt. 7:7–8).

3. We confessed our sins to God. Here again, we used scriptural statements. We also shared in our own words our human failures. We confessed our lack of faith. We claimed forgiveness based upon John's wonderful promise in 1 John 1:9.

4. We were very specific in our prayers. At this point in the process, we asked God to lead us to people who could help us—both Christians and non-Christians. We reminded the Lord that if He could use Artaxerxes, we believed that there were people in Dallas who could help us if God moved on their hearts and gave us opportunity to make our needs known.

We also asked for miraculous financial resources, for ours were very limited. We were a small group of people, and no one among us was considered wealthy. We hardly had enough income to pay the rent on our facility from week to week and to take care of some part-time salaries. We were praying for a miracle! At that moment, we felt that we had exhausted every human resource.

The Miracle Happened

God answered our prayers in ways that were far beyond what we imagined. We were overwhelmed with His grace. Please understand that it didn't happen all at once. We also faced one difficult barrier after another. But over a period of time, God unfolded a plan that was absolutely supernatural. I'll share what happened in the next chapter for it correlates dramatically with Nehemiah's experience with answered prayer.

Becoming a Man of Prayer

As you evaluate the following principles, pray and ask the Holy Spirit to impress on your heart one or two lessons that you need to apply more effectively in your own prayer life. Then write out a specific goal. For example, you may never have bypassed a need in your own life in order to spend time in prayer. Or, you've never really been persistent in prayer.

➤ We must pray out of a heart of deep concern.

➤ We must make prayer a priority over other needs.

➤ We must pray persistently.

➤ We must recognize that God is great and awesome.

➤ We should also remind God of His promises to us.

➤ We must acknowledge our unworthiness and sinfulness, our human weaknesses and failings.

➤ We must be specific in our prayers if we want to get specific answers.

Set a Goal

With God's help, I will begin immediately to carry out the following goal in my life:

_____

_____

_____

_____

Memorize the Following Scripture

Do not be anxious about anything, but in everything, by prayer and petition, with thanksgiving, present your requests to God. And the peace of God, which transcends all understanding, will guard your hearts and your minds in Christ Jesus.
                                        PHILIPPIANS 4:6–7, NIV

Chapter 2

Walking the Tight Rope
Read Nehemiah 2:1–8

*H*ave you ever hoped for good news and received bad news? All of us have at some moment in our lives. It's always disappointing! But few of us have experienced the crushing blow and emotional pain that Nehemiah experienced when he received a report on the status of his fellow Jews in Jerusalem.

Broken Walls and Intense Despair!

What Nehemiah had hoped *would not happen,* but feared *would happen, actually happened!* The wall that circled Jerusalem was in a shambles and the city gates had been "burned with fire." His fellow Jews were in "great distress and reproach." Their despair was intense and enormous. Their morale was at an all-time low. The news was so dismal that Nehemiah went into a state of deep depression (see Neh. 1:4).

Strange as it may seem, Nehemiah was probably not completely caught off guard. Many Bible scholars believe that Artaxerxes—the king he served as cupbearer—had actually issued a decree sometime earlier to thwart the Jews in their efforts to rebuild the wall in Jerusalem.[1] If this assumption is correct—and I believe it is—then Nehemiah had to presume that things were not going well for his fellow Jews. But being human and deeply concerned about his people, he was not ready emotionally to handle this bad news. We never are—no matter how much we try to prepare ourselves intellectually.

A Damaging Letter

Rehum—a Persian official in Samaria—had written to Artaxerxes to inform him that the Jews he had allowed to return to Jerusalem were rebuilding the city and were actually "finishing the walls and repairing the foundations" (Ezra 4:12). "Let it be known to the king," he reported, "that if that city is rebuilt and the walls are finished, they will not pay tribute, custom, or toll, and it will damage the revenue of the kings" (v. 13).

Understandably, this letter got Artaxerxes' attention. After researching the history of Jerusalem, he quickly recognized what might happen if the Jews succeeded in their efforts. He responded with a letter of his own and issued a command to stop the work (see v. 21). No sooner had Rehum received the king's response, he "went in haste to Jerusalem to the Jews and stopped them by force of arms" (v. 23).

The Devastating Results

Rehum and his cohorts must have literally attacked the walls of Jerusalem and broken them down and set the gates on fire. No wonder the Jews were demoralized. Years of hard work went up in smoke!

I can't help but remember my first visit to Warsaw, Poland. My wife and I sat in a little theater and looked at a movie that contained actual footage of the German forces attacking this beautiful city. Not only did the Nazis bomb the city from the air, but their ground attack was even more devastating. They went from building to building and literally destroyed each structure with dynamite. The whole city was in a shambles. Hitler's strategy was to break the morale of the Polish people and he calculated that he could accomplish this goal by destroying

Warsaw—the seat of Polish pride and their sense of accomplishment.

Rehum's strategy was similar—and it worked. His attack on Jerusalem was devastating to the Jews' morale. Emotionally, they were totally demoralized.

How Much Did Nehemiah Actually Know?

Because of Nehemiah's powerful and key position in the king's courts, he *must* have known about Rehum's initial letter and Artaxerxes' response. However, he apparently had not heard what had happened—though he probably feared that Rehum would not be kind to the Jews. He expected a bad report but nothing as devastating as what actually happened.

Nehemiah knew instantly that he faced what appeared to be an impossible task. From a human point of view, Artaxerxes was the only person who could help solve the problem. He had issued the order to stop the building process in the first place, and he would be the only one who could reverse it. This explains why Nehemiah prayed so specifically and asked God to "grant him compassion before this man" (Neh. 1:11).

A Miraculous Opportunity

Nehemiah's opportunity (2:1–2) came four months after he began to fast and pray—from Chislev (November–December) to Nisan (March–April). Evidently, Nehemiah was serving at a special banquet since the queen was at Artaxerxes' side (see v. 6).

Nehemiah was performing his usual duties. But there was something uniquely different about his countenance on this occasion. This was the first time he had ever looked dejected in the king's presence. "Why is your face sad though you are not sick?" the king inquired. Artaxerxes sensed immediately that something was seriously wrong and with penetrating insight, he answered his own question—"This is nothing but sadness of heart" (v. 2).

A Scary Moment

Nehemiah was frightened—and understandably so! It was against Persian law for a servant ever to show sadness in the king's presence. In fact, Nehemiah knew that he was in danger of being severely punished for demonstrating anything but a joyful countenance while on duty. He could have been demoted—or even imprisoned—which would make it virtually impossible for him to seek help from the king.

I'm confident Nehemiah knew the risk he was taking. But he had no choice. In a spirit of prayer and trusting God, he let his guard down, hoping the king would notice and not respond negatively.

More importantly, Nehemiah had to be thinking about the heavy-duty responsibility that lay on his shoulders. What if the king actually responded favorably to his deep concern? What would he say to the man who had issued an earlier order causing the very condition that had broken Nehemiah's spirit?

It's obvious that Nehemiah had been thinking and praying long and hard about this moment that finally arrived. Though Artaxerxes' comments frightened him, he was ready with his response. "Let the king live forever," he answered, assuring Artaxerxes of his personal loyalty. But then, he dealt with the real issue with great wisdom. "Why should my face not be sad when the *city*, the place of my *fathers' tombs*, lies desolate and its gates have been consumed by fire?" (v. 3).

Nehemiah Did Not Identify the "City" by Name

This may sound like a simple, naive response. Not so! Nehemiah demonstrated great wisdom. He avoided putting Artaxerxes on the defensive by not mentioning Jerusalem specifically. He simply called it a "city." After all, the king had investigated the history of Jerusalem—perhaps somewhat recently. What he discovered troubled him so deeply he had issued an order against the city so it couldn't be rebuilt (see Ezra 4:19–20). This was not the time to threaten Artaxerxes.

An Appeal to the King's Respect for Ancestors

Nehemiah knew Artaxerxes had a great sense of reverence for relatives and friends who had died. This mentality permeated the Middle Eastern culture.

Again we see Nehemiah's wisdom. He was hoping to strike a sensitive and responsive chord in Artaxerxes' heart. This is why he answered the king's inquiry about his sadness by stating that no one could be happy if the city and place of his *"father's tombs lies desolate."*

The "Moment of Truth"

Imagine Nehemiah's state of mind. Under these conditions, seconds can seem like hours. He must have waited with bated breath for the king's answer—with questions flooding his mind.

➤ Would he be severely punished for losing emotional control in the king's presence?

➤ Would he be transferred to another position—eliminating what seemed to be the only possibility for helping his fellow Jews in Jerusalem?

➤ Would the king even take his concerns seriously and pursue the matter further?

The king's response must have sent chills up and down Nehemiah's spine. Rather than bellowing with anger and charging his guards to remove Nehemiah, Artaxerxes responded positively. "What would you request?" asked the king (Neh. 2:4).

Nehemiah knew that a great door of opportunity had just been cracked opened. And he also knew he needed more divine wisdom to open it wide enough to walk through. While attempting to formulate an answer to Artaxerxes' critical question, Nehemiah quickly and silently whispered a prayer to God for help (see v. 4).

We're not told the specific content of his prayer. Personally, I would have certainly asked for both strength in my knees as well as wisdom to express my thoughts and desires clearly. At a time like this, it's easy to go blank and forget everything. Fear does amazing things to the brain. I'm confident Nehemiah faced the same emotional trauma.

Nehemiah Had Done His Homework

Though God certainly gave Nehemiah wisdom in the midst of what was happening, it's apparent that he had prepared for this golden opportunity (vv. 5–8). It's probably more accurate to conclude that at that moment, God gave Nehemiah the ability to use the knowledge he had gleaned from his days and weeks of careful research.

This is a powerful lesson for all of us. Nehemiah had not only prayed and sought God's help but he used all of the human resources that were available—including his intellectual skills, his human experiences, his accumulated wisdom, his role and position, and the people with whom he came in contact.

An Intricate Balance

Nehemiah carefully and wisely blended both divine and human resources to achieve his goals. He had prayed specifically for an opportunity to win a hearing with Artaxerxes (see 1:4–11). The opportunity came—and when it did, he again sought God's help (see 2:4). But he'd also prepared himself intellectually for this moment—which is clear from the way he answered the king's questions. As the conversation continued, the extent to which Nehemiah had prepared becomes more and more apparent. This is particularly obvious by his bold request.

"What Would You Request?"

Artaxerxes' straightforward and pointed question must have temporarily stunned Nehemiah. But with God's help, he regained his equilibrium and made a bold request. He asked the king to send him to Judah—the "city" of his "fathers' tombs" that he might "rebuild it" (v. 5). Responding boldly, but cautiously, Nehemiah once again referred to ancestral respect and once again he avoided naming the city of Jerusalem.

Artaxerxes Was No Fool

By now, the king certainly knew what city Nehemiah was referring to. In fact, he probably saw through Nehemiah's strategy early on. But because Nehemiah had been so wise with his nonthreatening approach, Artaxerxes admired his faithful servant. Remember, too, that Nehemiah had already won the king's trust. He had never given Artaxerxes a single reason to question his integrity and loyalty. If he had, he would not have been serving as the king's cupbearer.

A Reputation Worth Working For

What a great lesson this is for all of us! There's no substitute for a good reputation when it comes to asking for special favors. Many a person has been bypassed in a promotion or has even been demoted because of mistakes that have caused others to question his integrity and trustworthiness. It often takes years to develop this kind of reputation and trust—but when the moment comes, it's worth every bit of effort we've exerted to be "above reproach" (1 Tim. 3:2; Titus 1:6). This kind of lifestyle will pay rich dividends. It certainly did for Nehemiah!

Another Subtle Factor

Remember that the queen was sitting at Artaxerxes' side (see Neh. 2:6). This complicated matters for Nehemiah. If she had been listening in on this very sensitive conversation and heard the name "Jerusalem," she would have found it very easy to remind the king of his earlier decision—which would certainly have threatened his male ego. If this had happened, it would have been much more difficult for King Artaxerxes to respond positively to Nehemiah's request. We can now understand more clearly why Nehemiah had to word his responses very carefully. In circumstances like this, just one word misspoken can destroy a unique opportunity.

A Wide Open Door

Nehemiah obviously cleared this hurdle. There is no evidence the queen even commented. This, too, must have brought a sigh of relief.

The king's next question threw "the door wide open"—a question that set the stage for Nehemiah to share some requests he'd been thinking about for a long time. "How long will your journey be," the king asked, "and when will you return?" (v. 6).

In thinking through the whole process ahead of time, Nehemiah knew that a trip to Jerusalem without the king's special permission as well as his personal resources would fail. Even if he arrived safely, there wouldn't be much he could do for his fellow Jews.

Letters of Permission

First of all, Nehemiah requested letters of permission from the king himself to allow him to pass through the various provinces. He needed these letters to be able to reach Jerusalem without opposition (see v. 7). Nehemiah knew that the only way he would be permitted to cross borders was to have these letters from the king—for every governor along the way would have been aware of the king's previous letter to stop the Jews from rebuilding the city of Jerusalem.

Access to the King's Forest

Second, Nehemiah asked for a letter to Asaph, the man who was in charge of the king's forest. It wasn't a coincidence that Nehemiah knew that one of the king's forests was near Jerusalem. Even more amazing, he actually knew the *name* of the man who was in charge. In unlocking this door, Nehemiah knew he would have access to materials to rebuild the walls and other parts of the city (see v. 8).

The Key to Success

Nehemiah himself describes the "key" that opened this marvelous door of opportunity. After being granted positive answers to his bold requests, he said, "And the king granted them to me *because the good hand of my God was on me*" (v. 8). Though Nehemiah had worked hard preparing himself for the opportunity to share his burden with the king, and though he was able to demonstrate unusual wisdom in responding to the king's questions, when all was said and done, he knew his success happened because of God's help. As we'll see in future chapters, this quality of life characterized Nehemiah throughout his entire ministry.

Becoming God's Man Today

Principles to Live By

One of the greatest lessons we can learn from Nehemiah's approach to leadership is to balance divine and human factors—no matter what our task. This principle applies to all aspects of our lives—in leading our families, in operating our businesses, and as participants in our churches. We've already seen this balance in Nehemiah's life. On the one hand, he had prayed, seeking God's help, realizing it was impossible in his own strength for him to solve the problem he faced. On the other hand, he worked hard to do everything he could to prepare himself for the moment God would open the door to the king's mind and heart.

Principle 1. At times, we may not be as effective as we should be because we do not do all we can to prepare ourselves for our tasks.

I'm convinced that opportunities come and pass us by because we're not properly equipped to take advantage of those opportunities. In some instances, we may not even recognize the opportunity. But if we do, we often don't have the knowledge, the emotional stamina, or the skills to do what we must do in order to succeed.

A Disappointing Experience

I remember serving with a pastor who spent a great deal of time in prayer. I admire that quality. However, among other things, he refused to spend time strategizing to reach new people.

On one occasion, I worked very hard to plan an evening of outreach—a time to visit new people in our community and invite them to visit our church. He and his wife came to the dinner we had in our home prior to going out to meet new people. However, after the dinner, the pastor and his wife excused themselves, told us they'd be praying for us—and then left. Frankly, I was devastated since I'd worked diligently, not only to prepare the group for this opportunity but to also make it easy for the pastor to participate.

Please don't misunderstand! Being a pastor myself, I'm well aware that we may, as spiritual leaders, have other pressing responsibilities—people who need crisis counseling, messages that we need to prepare, family priorities, etc. But, in this situation, this was not the case. This was the story of this man's life. He believed that prayer by itself would reach new people. He didn't believe that God needed our human effort to reach out and make contacts.

A Classic Model

Nehemiah was also a man of prayer. But he teaches us that relying on prayer alone is never God's way of achieving His goals on earth. Merely trusting Him as the sovereign of the universe is a very superficial theological approach. God is indeed sovereign, but He has placed on all of us significant human responsibilities.

True, it's sometimes difficult to balance these two concepts pragmatically. However, it's absolutely essential that we maintain this balance in order to be effective. This balance is illustrated again and again in the Scriptures—and Nehemiah is a classic model.

Principle 2. At times, we may not be as effective as we should be because we are trying to do everything in our own strength.

This is the other extreme—the "peril of the pendulum"! At times, we fail as husbands, as fathers, as businessmen, as churchmen—because we take matters into our own hands. We don't seek God's help. We rely on our own human wisdom and skills.

True, we may use the words *prayer* and *faith*, but they are merely that—"words." We're saying the right thing, but we're still attempting to solve problems more humanistically than spiritually.

It's not easy to maintain this balance. It's a constant challenge. It's more natural to go to extremes.

The Rest of the Story

God does answer prayer. With Him, even the impossible becomes possible.

At the end of the previous chapter, I shared the beginning of a story. As a small group of Christians in Dallas, we faced our own "Jerusalem" experience. Our "walls were broken down." Translated into modern language, we believed God wanted us to establish a church in the Park Cities area of Dallas but property was scarce and expensive. The picture was bleak and discouraging.

We'd looked for property for a year and a half. Yes, we had also prayed—but not like Nehemiah. And then we decided to follow his example. One Sunday evening in our regular service

➤ we acknowledged God's greatness;

➤ we reminded Him of His promises;

➤ we confessed our sins and claimed forgiveness in Christ;

➤ we prayed specifically, asking God to do what seemed to be the impossible (to review this process in more detail, see pp. 16–18).

I'll never forget my feelings as we concluded that evening of corporate prayer and praise. I was driving home with my wife, and my faith suddenly seemed to dissipate. I had a lump in my throat and a knot in my stomach. "What have I done?" I asked my wife. "What if nothing happens? What if I have led these people into a high level of expectancy only to see their hopes dashed?"

What happened next demonstrates why we need corporate prayer. God gave me the faith to lead this group through the process—and then when my faith failed, others kept on believing. In fact, God was already answering our prayers. That very evening, a woman I had never met before was visiting for the first time. I didn't even know she was there until I received a call the next day from the man for whom she worked. He volunteered to meet with me to talk about our concern for property.

Would you believe the woman who was visiting was this man's secretary—and when she got to work the next day, she shared with him what she'd experienced the evening before. She reiterated my message on Nehemiah's prayer process and observed how we had applied his approach to our own situation. I learned later that she had commented to her boss, "Those people practice true Christianity. They really believe God answers prayer!" I was thrilled, of course, with this feedback. Obviously, this newcomer had sensed our deep concern and faith.

My initial meeting with this man led to another meeting with several of our elders. John volunteered to do everything he could to help us find property. We attempted to turn over every stone—to explore every possibility. But with each idea, we seemed to hit a blank wall. Finally, our new friend asked us if we had talked with a particular home builder who was constructing homes on the Caruth homestead. One of our men responded that he had approached this man approximately a year ago and was told that there was no possibility to get land for a church.

You need to understand that this particular homestead was a large undeveloped and choice piece of property located in the center of Dallas. It bordered Central Expressway—a main artery. To the immediate west and southwest of this property were the Park Cities—our target area. To the north was the expansive North Park Shopping Center. In fact, this homestead was the only major undeveloped section of land in that area.

We agreed that we needed to talk to the developer again. We were surprised—even shocked—when he responded positively. He showed us a two-and-a-half-acre plot he would consider relinquishing so that we could build our church. God worked another miracle when the other principals agreed to the deal—for a price that was far under the normal value of the property.

Even then, the price was enormous for our small group. The Lord had brought us this far, and we knew He would continue to open doors. Incidentally, after we closed the deal, the property shortly thereafter doubled and tripled in value.

At the time, we didn't really understand how great a miracle this was. We were later told that if we had contacted this developer one week earlier or one week later, it probably would have been impossible to secure the land. This only added to the divine nature and timing of our prayer process and the results. Frankly, I felt like I was reliving Nehemiah's experience. Though what was happening to us could not compare in magnitude to Nehemiah's predicament, for us it seemed just as magnificent.

This was just the beginning of one miracle after another—from financing to completing the project. At one point, we almost lost the property because of a feud between two developers, but because two Christian women "just happened" to be on the Dallas city council when the vote was taken, we were given permission to proceed.

Another Miracle

Since that time, the church has grown and has reached thousands of people. A good friend of mine, Bill Counts, became senior pastor, and my wife and I moved on to start Fellowship Bible Church North in Plano, Texas—the church I presently serve as senior pastor.

Under Bill's leadership, the work continued to grow and expand until it could no longer handle the flow of people—even though they were conducting four identical services every weekend. And then they experienced another miracle! They were able to sell the property to a smaller group of Christians and were able to purchase a large business complex that became available because of the real estate recession.

One of the most amazing aspects of all of this is that God used the same Christian developer who had helped us to get the initial tract of land in the Caruth homestead to work out the details regarding the business complex. Today, the church has unlimited potential to expand and reach people for Christ. All this began with—and resulted from—a small group of believers practicing the Nehemiah prayer process.

Becoming a Man of Wisdom

To what extent are you balancing divine and human factors in your life? Are you laying back and waiting for God to do it all? Or are you trying to do it all by yourself?

You can avoid these extremes. Begin now—today—to commit yourself to discovering that balance moment by moment, day by day, and week by week—as you live for God in this world.

As you reflect on the following guidelines, pray and ask the Holy Spirit to impress on your heart at least one lesson you need to apply more effectively to maintain this unique balance. Then write out a specific goal. For example, you may need to seek advice from other mature members of Christ's body to help you maintain this balance.

> ➤ Consult the Word of God regularly.

> ➤ In times of uncertainty and crisis, use Nehemiah's prayer process no matter what your concerns—be they large or small.

> ➤ Seek advice from other mature members of Christ's body.

> ➤ Evaluate circumstances carefully, but do not allow them to discourage you. What may appear to be impossible may indeed be possible with God's help.

> ➤ Interpret your own personal "feelings" about the matter carefully. On the one hand, feelings of confidence may reflect a sense of pride. On the other hand, feelings of distress may reflect natural and normal reactions.

Remember this! If Nehemiah had followed his feelings, he would have given up! And I must admit, if I had followed my feelings when we were facing an enormous crisis in trying to start this new church, I would have given up too! I'm so thankful I discovered Nehemiah's model prayer.

Set a Goal

With God's help, I will begin immediately to carry out the following goal in my life:

_____

_____

_____

_____

_____

_____

Memorize the Following Scripture

Now to Him who is able to do exceeding abundantly beyond all that we ask or think, according to the power that works within us, to Him be the glory in the church and in Christ Jesus to all generations forever and ever. Amen.

EPHESIANS 3:20–21

Chapter 3

God's Hands—Our Hands
Read Nehemiah 2:9–20

A university president once said that there are three kinds of people in the world:

> ➤ those who don't know what is happening,
> ➤ those who watch what's happening, and
> ➤ those who make things happen!

Without question, Nehemiah *made* things happen! But when things happened, it was not only because of his human ingenuity and his hard work. Rather, it was God's blessing blended with diligence. Nehemiah understood this truth. When King Artaxerxes gave him letters to cross borders and a letter of access to the official forest outside of Jerusalem, Nehemiah responded by saying, "And the king granted them to me *because the good hand of my God was on me*" (2:8).

More Than He Asked For

Nehemiah had experienced an incredible miracle (vv. 9–10). In fact, when he asked Artaxerxes for official letters to permit him to cross various borders as well as for the special letter to Asaph to give him access to the king's forest, Nehemiah actually received more than he asked for. In addition to these concessions, the king also ordered his military officers to escort Nehemiah safely all the way to Jerusalem (see v. 9).

Can you imagine the excitement that must have gripped Nehemiah's heart? This additional blessing was totally unexpected. After months of praying, mourning, and fasting as he faced a seemingly impossible task, he now found himself square in the middle of the king's escort headed for Jerusalem. In his hands were official letters signed and sealed by Artaxerxes himself. This was a miracle!

The trip to Jerusalem wasn't a weekend excursion. It took at least two months. Even before he arrived, the word was out that he was coming. Israel's enemies were definitely not happy about the situation—"And when Sanballat the Horonite and Tobiah the Ammonite official heard about it, it was very displeasing to them that someone had come to seek the welfare of the sons of Israel" (v. 10).

Even though Nehemiah knew he wasn't welcome, he remained undaunted. He knew God had brought him to this moment in Israel's history. He'd experienced too many miracles to begin to doubt now. At the same time, he knew he was about to tackle a gigantic project that others before him—for almost 150 years—had been unable to complete.

A Secret Survey

Even though his two-month journey must have been terribly exhausting, Nehemiah went right to work when he arrived in Jerusalem (vv. 11–16). We're told he "was there three days" (v. 11). It certainly wouldn't take this long to verify that the report he had received six months earlier was true. Morale was at an all-time low. Discouragement permeated the ranks of Israel.

Long Days and Sleepless Nights

During those three days, Nehemiah apparently didn't sleep very much—perhaps a few hours until all was quiet in the city.

He probably spent the daytime hours asking questions, getting to know the people, and evaluating their status. During the night hours, he inspected the walls and surveyed the damage.

Nehemiah quickly discerned that he couldn't let the people at large know immediately why he was there and what God wanted him to do—at least without doing some very careful research and planning. Part of that plan was to take a few men that he could trust into his confidence.

> And I arose in the night, I and a few men with me. I did not tell anyone what my God was putting in my mind to do for Jerusalem and there was no animal with me except the animal on which I was riding. . . . And the officials did not know where I had gone or what I had done; nor had I as yet told the Jews, the priests, the nobles, the officials, or the rest who did the work. (vv. 12, 16)

Nehemiah's Greatest Challenge

Surveying the wall and coming up with a rebuilding plan evidently was not a difficult task for Nehemiah (vv. 17–20). He accomplished this in three nights. His greatest challenge was to convince the people to tackle this project. It's one thing to get excited about a difficult challenge when things are going well; it's another thing to get excited when you're discouraged and ready to give up. This was the situation Nehemiah faced.

In spite of their low morale, Nehemiah hit the problem head-on. He challenged the people: "Come, let us rebuild the wall of Jerusalem that we may no longer be a reproach" (v. 17).

Overcoming Negativism

Imagine the negative thoughts and feelings that must have gripped the hearts of the Jews when they heard Nehemiah's challenge. First, they'd be skeptical. Who is this guy? Where did he come from? Who does he think he is? And rebuild the walls! Doesn't he understand what we're facing? He's asking us to do the impossible!

Like most of us, in similar circumstances, we would think Nehemiah was either crazy or on some kind of ego trip! We would have viewed Nehemiah's challenge as an impossible task.

Leading Proactively

Nehemiah was no novice when it came to understanding people and their feelings. He certainly had anticipated their negative reactions. Apparently, before his people could even voice their negative feelings, Nehemiah went on to report how God had already helped him. "And I told them," he later wrote, "how the hand of my God had been favorable to me, and also about the king's words which he had spoken to me" (v. 18).

At some point during Nehemiah's report, negative feelings turned positive. Despair turned to hope. They believed Nehemiah and trusted him.

"Let Us Arise and Build!"

We're not told how long this whole communication process took. But knowing the magnitude of the challenge in the midst of some very intense feelings of despair, the leaders in Israel must have spent some quality time interacting with Nehemiah—and then communicating their own consensus to the people. Whatever happened, Nehemiah succeeded in getting his message through. Together and with enthusiasm, the people responded and said, "Let us arise and build." And that's exactly what they did. Nehemiah later reported in his journal that the people "put their hands to the good work" (v. 18). Nehemiah had rallied the people to "roll up their sleeves," put their "shoulders to the wheel," and attack what they believed was an impossible task.

God's Hands at Work Through Human Hands

Again we see the interrelatedness between God's enablement and man's involvement. Nehemiah had reported that he had been successful because God's hand was on him (see v. 8). And now in verse 18 we read that "the people put *their hands* to the good work." This is the way it has always been when God's people are achieving true spiritual objectives. *God's hands* are at work through *human hands.*

Facing the Enemy with Confidence

Word regarding Israel's decision to rebuild the walls under Nehemiah's leadership spread rapidly. To counter this plan, the enemies of Israel stepped up their own efforts to undermine Nehemiah's efforts. They "mocked" the children of Israel and "despised" them. They used every demoralizing technique they could think of—including the earlier decree ordered by King Artaxerxes. Even though Sanballat and Tobiah must have known that this decree had been reversed and Nehemiah had been granted permission by the king to rebuild the wall, they tried to use outdated information to achieve their own selfish goals (see v. 19).

Nehemiah was not intimidated by their insidious attacks. He faced their verbal abuse with bold words of his own. "The God of heaven will give us success," he stated. "We . . . *will* arise and build, but you have no portion, right, or memorial in Jerusalem" (v. 20).

God's Strength—Our Strength

Nehemiah's balanced perspective on the human and divine was one of his strongest traits as a spiritual leader. He let his enemies know that he and the children of Israel were "servants" *of God.* He also let them know that *they would* "arise and build." With this bold statement, he was letting both the children of Israel and his enemies know that their dependence was not primarily on their human abilities, their human resources, or their personal genius. Their hope was in the God of Abraham, Isaac, and Jacob—who had promised them the city of Jerusalem. At the same time, Nehemiah's words flowed from a sense of confidence that he and his people had the ability to accomplish this superhuman task.

Becoming God's Man Today

Principles to Live By

The powerful principle we learn from Nehemiah's initial days in Jerusalem is the same basic principle illustrated when Nehemiah first approached Artaxerxes that evening when he was performing his duties in the king's court.

Principle 1. We must strive to maintain a proper balance between divine and human factors as we carry out our God-given responsibilities.

Nehemiah had prepared himself thoroughly for that moment when Artaxerxes asked him about his dejected countenance. He had well-thought-out answers on the tip of his tongue. Even when he was responding to Artaxerxes' additional questions, he was quietly praying for divine guidance in order to respond wisely.

The same thing happened in Nehemiah's life once he arrived in Jerusalem. If he were going to be able to convince the children of Israel that they should "arise and build," he knew that he needed to prepare thoroughly a strategy in advance and then carefully, but confidently, unveil that plan with discretion and wisdom.

But Nehemiah also knew that an ingenious plan alone would not turn the tide. He had to convince the children of Israel that this task could be accomplished with God's help. To get this point across, he shared with them his own experience with Artaxerxes several months before.

They knew Nehemiah had to be telling the truth. What other explanation would there be for his presence in Jerusalem? Furthermore, he had evidence—official letters signed by the king himself. And somewhere a group of military men were stationed—the king's horsemen who had escorted him all the way to Jerusalem.

We must continually exert *conscious effort* to maintain a proper balance between *relying upon God* and *using our own human talents and abilities.*

Maintaining this balance in itself calls for "human effort." It doesn't happen automatically. God places a significant amount of responsibility on us. In this sense, the scale that so intricately balances God's sovereignty and human responsibility is weighted in our direction. We are responsible to take the initiative.

Don't Misunderstand

I'm not suggesting that our efforts take precedence over God's sovereign plans. But from a practical point of view, we're responsible to utilize the divine and supernatural resources He's given us. In that sense, He has *already* taken the initiative.

➤ We have His revealed will in the Scriptures.

➤ We have the presence of the Holy Spirit in our lives.

➤ We have that marvelous resource known as prayer—which we've seen so dramatically illustrated in Nehemiah's life.

God has also provided us with many human and natural resources—other mature Christians, libraries filled with knowledge and wisdom, our own intelligence, and experiential backgrounds. But we are the ones who must decide whether or not we're going to use these divine and human resources. God has not promised to resolve automatically our problems without intensive effort on our part. Even Bible study and prayer involves self-discipline and personal sacrifice.

Reflect for a moment on what we've learned from Nehemiah that illustrates this truth. He spent many weeks fasting and praying—preparing for the moment when he was asked that critical question by Artaxerxes. Because he was ready to respond with wisdom and insight, it affected the course of Israel's history.

A Twentieth-Century Illustration

This problem of balancing the human and the divine became very clear to me one day when I served as a full-time professor at Dallas Theological Seminary. I was participating in a faculty discussion regarding a projected multimillion-dollar campus development program. To test the waters, we had sent out some initial communication to friends of the seminary, explaining our intent and asking for feedback and support. The response was meager.

These results would not be surprising to those involved in fund-raising, particularly if they evaluated our initial mail-out. It was a simple letter—no colorful brochures and a few details. But one faculty member—who was well known for his strong views on God's sovereign control of the universe and who was usually rather verbal against any kind of promotional effort—spoke out forthrightly. "It appears God is telling us not to build since we're getting so little financial response from our friends." At that time, I was a junior member of the faculty but I couldn't help responding in the same outspoken manner. "It may also indicate," I said, "that we have failed to do *our part* in letting people know how important this project really is to our future effectiveness."

The facts are that once we began to do a better job in the promotional and development areas of our school, people began to respond. Since that day—a number of years ago—a great campus has been built comprised of numerous up-to-date structures. God honored our human efforts that were combined with prayer and faith in Him. At the same time, God worked in the hearts of people to respond to our communication.

A Delicate Balance

Please don't misunderstand. And please don't be too hard on my fellow professor—or me! I, too, firmly believe in God's sovereignty. He *does* control our affairs. But I also know that the Bible is filled with illustrations and instructions regarding human responsibility. And I also know from biblical examples and personal experiences that how we respond to opportunities that lie before us and what we do as God's children to realize these opportunities does make a difference.

Take Nehemiah, for Instance

While in Susa, he could have prayed rather than *prepare* when he received the report from Jerusalem. If he had not done his homework, he would not have been ready to face Artaxerxes' interrogation.

When he arrived in Jerusalem, he could have also prayed and trusted God and not surveyed the walls by night which enabled him to prepare an incredible plan. Again, if he had only prayed—and not done his part—the people would have been horribly frustrated. The project would have failed, unless God raised up another man who would both "pray and prepare"—which He would have done because of His *sovereign plan* and His *unconditional promises* to Israel.

What about That Faculty Discussion?

What I've just shared about Nehemiah applies to the discussion we were having about a campus development program. If we had listened to the professor who concluded that lack of response indicated that it wasn't God's will to proceed, the project would never have gotten off the drawing board. There would be no new buildings to help the present faculty carry out that great ministry at Dallas Theological Seminary.

I want to hasten to say that if our efforts had not been bathed in prayer, if we had not trusted God and sought His will in the Word of God, the project might never have been possible either. If we had succeeded in doing it without God's help—which is possible—we would be merely building a monument to man rather than to God. Furthermore, if we had not maintained an intricate balance, God's ultimate blessings would not be upon us.

Principle 2. It is our responsibility as Christians to maintain unity in the body of Christ.

A New Testament Example

The apostle Paul's concern for unity among Christians illustrates the application of this powerful principle. There's no question that all Christians who put their faith in Christ are one in Christ. Paul clearly made this point when he described the relationship between Jews and Gentiles once they became believers. Writing to the Ephesians—and speaking specifically to the Gentile believers—he said: "Remember that you were at that time [before your conversion] separate from Christ, excluded from the commonwealth of Israel, and strangers to the covenants of promise, having no hope and without God in the world. But now in Christ Jesus you who formerly were far off have been brought near by the blood of Christ" (Eph. 2:12–13). Paul then continued by saying that Christ has broken down the dividing wall so that "He might make the two into *one new man* . . . and might reconcile them *both in one body*" (vv. 15–16).

All Christians are one in Christ. If Paul is telling the truth—which we definitely believe he is—this oneness is automatic when we accept Christ as our personal Lord and Savior. God does it all! We're adopted into His family!

However, this unity exists in God's heart and mind. It's a theological reality. Describing it in another way, it's "positional truth." But in this historical setting—among the Christians in Ephesus and throughout Asia—this doctrinal reality still needed to be applied in the lives of these first-century Christians. If they were actually living as if they were already truly one, Paul would not have had to exhort them to be "diligent to preserve the unity of the Spirit in the bond of peace" (4:3).

The rest of Paul's letter to the Ephesians is filled with instructions on how to develop and maintain this oneness. It would only happen if these believers did everything they could to bring it about.

Responsibility for practical and visible unity in the church lies squarely on the shoulders of all of us who are followers of Jesus Christ.

Becoming a Balanced Man

It's true that these great biblical realities are difficult to comprehend and reconcile in our finite minds. God's sovereignty and man's free will remain a great mystery—an antinomy. Both are true, but they cannot be easily defined and explained.

From a purely human perspective, they appear to be irreconcilable concepts. And have you noticed that those who spend countless hours trying to understand and explain these great truths frequently go to extremes, ignoring one point of view or the other?

As you read through the following "pairs of statements," evaluate your own approach to Bible interpretation and Christian living. Once you've completed this exercise, then write out a specific goal. For example, you may discover that you are overly focused on "God's sovereign control" of the universe. On the other hand, you may discover you are overly focused on "human responsibility."

Each statement in the following "pairs" reflects a point of view. Check to see if your personal views fall into one category or another.

1. ___When I read and study the Scriptures, I see primarily an emphasis on God's sovereign control of the universe.

   ___ When I read and study the Scriptures, I see primarily an emphasis on human responsibility.

2. ___ The concept of God's sovereignty is in my mind constantly.

   ___ The concept of human responsibility as a Christian is constantly in my thoughts.

3. ____ I tend to resent people who always talk about human responsibility.

____ I tend to resent people who always talk about God's sovereignty.

4. ____ I find it easy to withdraw from involvement in the lives of people because of my view of God's sovereignty.

____ I constantly have a sense of guilt because I do not have enough time in the day to do everything that needs to be done in carrying out God's work in the world.

5. ____ I am more concerned that Christians know about God's sovereign election for salvation than that they know they are responsible to carry out the Great Commission.

____ I am more concerned that Christians be involved in carrying out the Great Commission than that they understand God's sovereign election in salvation.

6. ____ I pray because God wants me to, though I really believe that what will happen will happen because of God's sovereign involvement in our lives.

____ If prayer does not change things, I believe it is because of a lack of faith on my part and an improper spiritual perspective.

7. ____ I do not believe that God will hold us responsible for people who eventually go to hell because they have never heard about Christ.

____ I believe that God will hold us responsible for the souls of those who go to hell and that their blood will be required at our hands.

8. ____ I believe that those who will be saved will be saved; that missionaries are not necessary.

____ I believe that people will be lost eternally because Christians have not shared the news of salvation through Jesus Christ.

If you checked most of the first items in each set of statements, you are probably going to an extreme regarding what the Bible teaches about God's "sovereignty." If you checked most of the second items in each set of statements, you are probably going to an extreme regarding our "human responsibility." If you had difficulty checking any of the statements, you are probably maintaining a proper balance.

Set a Goal

With God's help, I will begin immediately to carry out the following goal in my life:

_____

_____

_____

_____

_____

Memorize the Following Scripture

Oh, the depth of the riches both of the wisdom and knowledge of God! How unsearchable are His judgments and unfathomable His ways! For who has known the mind of the Lord, or who became His counselor? Or who has first given to Him that it might be paid back to Him again? For from Him and through Him and to Him are all things. To Him be the glory forever. Amen.
ROMANS 11:33–36

Chapter 4
<hr />

A Great Leadership Model
Read Nehemiah 3:1–32

I've had the privilege over the years of working with a number of key leaders—presidents, vice-presidents, pastors and their associates, managers, directors—and people with a variety of other titles. As I reflect, all of these people had certain strengths—otherwise they wouldn't have been in key leadership positions.

But as I reflected, I scratched my head to think of one who has measured up to the abilities and qualities of Nehemiah. He stands head and shoulders above us all! In that sense, he becomes a great model.

A Closer Look

It's easy to pass over this next chapter in Nehemiah's journal. Like a number of Old Testament accounts, it's filled with names that are difficult to pronounce, information that seems unusually redundant, and chronology that seems meaningless.

I've discovered that these observations and feelings only represent my human limitations. What we see in this chapter are the results of Nehemiah's nighttime survey—which resulted in a very ingenious plan. It also reflects Nehemiah's incredible leadership skills since he is recording what has already happened.

<hr />

To understand the details in this chapter, it's imperative that we *see* as well as *hear*. Note the map below. We're limited in archeological evidence, so the map merely *represents* the actual geographical setting—but it represents well the main outline Nehemiah used to record this section in his journal (see 3:1–32).

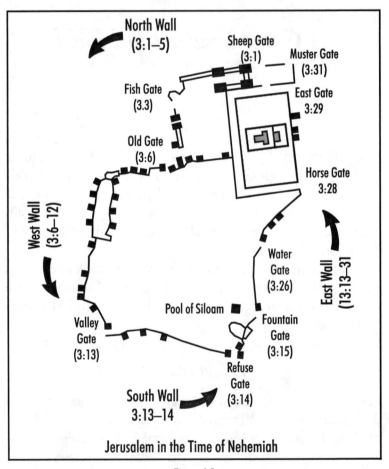

Jerusalem in the Time of Nehemiah

Figure 4-1

As you study this map, begin at "12:00" and move counter-clockwise, following the direction of the arrows. As you move around the wall, you'll notice that most of the specific places identified on the way are actually mentioned in chronological order in this chapter, beginning with the Sheep Gate in verse 1 and ending with the Inspection Gate in verse 31.

"Let's Get Organized"

Rebuilding the wall around Jerusalem was an enormous task—especially under such adverse conditions—and Nehemiah rose to the occasion. His organizational efforts are magnificent. He and his small band of men must have worked night and day putting this plan together.

Every Person Was in Place

Underscore in your Bible every time you see the following phrases in chapter 3: "next to him," "next to them," "after him," and "after them." You'll find these various phrases are recorded twenty-eight times in this chapter—in twenty-one of the thirty-two verses. For example, consider the following:

> Then Eliashib the high priest arose with his brothers the priests and built the Sheep Gate: they consecrated it and hung its doors. They consecrated the wall to the Tower of the Hundred and the Tower of Hananel.
>
> And *next to him* the men of Jericho built, and *next to them* Zaccur the son of Imri built.
>
> Now the sons of Hassenaah built the Fish Gate; they laid its beams and hung its doors with its bolts and bars.
>
> And *next to them* Meremoth the son of Uriah, the son of Hakkoz made repairs. And *next to him* Meshullam the son of Berechiah the son of Meshezabel made repairs. And *next to him* Zadok the son of Baana also made repairs.
>
> Moreover, *next to him* the Tekoites made repairs, but their nobles did not support the work of their masters. (vv. 1–5)

Nehemiah had a phenomenal ability to coordinate people—to get everyone involved. This didn't just happen. It *never* "just happens"! What may appear to be a smooth-running operation always reflects a lot of careful, behind-the-scenes planning.

Neither was this some spontaneous movement of God's Spirit that suddenly put every man and woman in a particular place around the wall, doing certain things. Rather, Nehemiah spent hours and hours doing careful research, analyzing the data, and putting it all together.

Remember, too, that once people were in their places, they needed careful supervision. They also needed adequate resources. Nehemiah thought through all of these things ahead of time.

This kind of coordination, of course, is preliminary to actually working the plan. This calls for highly effective communication.

People Were Assigned by Residence

As you look at the following statements, you can see Nehemiah's genius as a leader.

From the doorway of Eliashib's house even as far as *the end of his house.* . . .

After them Benjamin and Hasshub carried out repairs *in front of their house.* After them Azariah the son of Maaseiah, son of Ananiah carried out repairs *beside his house.*

After him Binnui the son of Henadad repaired another section, from the *house of Azariah.* . . .

Above the Horse Gate the priests carried out repairs, each *in front of his house.*

After them Zadok the son of Immer carried out repairs *in front of his house.* . . .

After him Meshullam the son of Berechiah carried out repairs *in front of his own quarters.* (vv. 21, 23–24, 28–30)

There are at least *four reasons* why Nehemiah developed this kind of coordinated plan:

1. People who were assigned to sections of the wall near their homes would be more personally involved and more highly motivated.

2. People would not have to travel to another part of the city to do the job, wasting valuable time.

3. In case of attack, these people would not be tempted to leave their posts, but would stay and protect their families.

4. The task would be a family effort, using all available talent.

All of this reflects incredible ingenuity—as Cyril Barber observes: "By arranging for each man to work close to his own home, Nehemiah made it easy for them to get to work, to be sustained while on the job, and to safeguard those who were nearest and dearest to them. This relieved each worker of any unnecessary anxiety. It also insured that each person would put his best effort into what he was doing."[1]

Assignments for Commuters

There were also a number of families who lived outside of Jerusalem—in Jericho, Tekoa, Gibeon, and Mizpah. Nehemiah assigned these men to sections of the wall where there weren't many homes (see vv. 2, 5, 7). They were asked to complete tasks that could not be as conveniently handled by the permanent residents in Jerusalem. Again, this was an ingenious plan! These people were involved but their location wasn't as critical in terms of protecting their families.

Assignment by Vocation

It appears that Nehemiah also assigned specific people to specific areas that related to their vocations. Though we don't have as much biblical evidence to illustrate this point, it was definitely true of the priests. Nehemiah assigned "Eliashib the high priest" and "his brothers" to rebuild the "Sheep Gate" (v. 1). This would be an assignment close to their own hearts, since it was through this gate that animals were brought to the temple for sacrifice.

We could probably find more clues in this chapter to point to Nehemiah's careful and cautious planning. However, we've looked at enough information to observe this man's unusual administrative skills.

"We've Got to Work Together"

We've already seen the positive response the children of Israel had to Nehemiah's plan. "Let us arise and build," they said (2:18). With few exceptions, everyone responded to Nehemiah's bold challenge. What we've just seen outlined in chapter 3 demonstrates conclusively that this initial response by the children of Israel was not just words. Neither were they motivated only by the "emotions" of the moment. They demonstrated their seriousness with their actions. They were not only hearers but doers—and most importantly, almost everyone was involved in this building project.

Those Who Were Experienced and Qualified

It's not surprising that a project like this called for leaders who were highly experienced and qualified to supervise the rebuilding of certain sections of the wall. In some instances, this probably involved the heads of households. But there were other sections of the wall that were rebuilt under the supervision of certain "officials" who were already experienced men in their own right. This is apparent from the following references:

> Rephaiah. . . , the *official* of half the district of Jerusalem, made repairs. . . .
>
> Shallum. . . , the *official* of half the district of Jerusalem, made repairs. . . .
>
> Malchijah . . . , the *official* of the district of Beth-haccherem, repaired the Refuse Gate. . . .
>
> Shallum . . . , the *official* of the district of Mizpah, repaired the Fountain Gate. . .
>
> Nehemiah . . . , *official* of half the district of Beth-zur, made repairs. . . .
>
> Hashabiah, the *official* of half the district of Keilah, carried out repairs for his district.
>
> Bavvai . . . , *official* of the other half of the district of Keilah.
>
> Ezer . . . , the *official* of Mizpah, repaired another section. (3:9, 12, 14–19)

A Particular Challenge

If you've ever worked with men and women in middle or top management positions, you'll quickly discover that these people are sometimes less cooperative with one another than people who do not have as much responsibility. There are a variety of reasons as to why this is true—but there is one primary reason. High-level management people are recognized in their own right as people with administrative abilities and skills. They are used to "giving orders" rather than "taking them."

The "officials" mentioned in this chapter apparently represent middle or top management people. Yet Nehemiah succeeded in getting all of these men to cooperate wholeheartedly in supervising the rebuilding of certain gates and sections of the wall. This was another unique leadership accomplishment.

All Ages—All Walks of Life

Nehemiah also succeeded in getting men and women of all ages and from all walks of life to participate in rebuilding the wall. There were "priests" (v. 1), "goldsmiths" (v. 8), "perfumers" (v. 8), "temple servants" (v. 26), and "merchants" (v. 32). What a cooperative effort!

Note also that Nehemiah mentioned that Shallum, an official of Jerusalem, worked side by side with "his daughters" (v. 12). How easy it would be to miss this bit of information. But it's very significant! It indicates that whole families worked together to rebuild certain sections of the wall.

A Few Exceptions

For the most part, everyone cooperated in this building project. There were, however, a few exceptions. There always are. Some people have good reasons for not participating, though others have poor reasons—or no reasons at all. Nehemiah faced this problem and he made note of it in his journal: "The Tekoites made repairs, but their nobles did not support the work of their masters" (v. 5).

Nehemiah doesn't tell us why these leaders refused to cooperate. Since they represent an elite group of individuals, maybe they felt they were above getting their hands dirty. Perhaps they didn't feel it was their responsibility since they lived outside of Jerusalem. They may not have been willing to make the sacrifice that would have been required. It could be that they were afraid to be identified with the children of Israel and face the same harassment from their enemies. Or, they may have been just plain selfish—or lazy. Whatever their reasons, they represent those few who always refuse to get involved in this kind of project.

Nehemiah didn't allow these negative responses to intimidate him or to interfere with his own desire to complete the task. After all, those who didn't cooperate were the exception—not the rule. The job was eventually completed in record time. Most everyone cooperated and did what they could, using their own skills, abilities, and resources.

We All Need Encouragement

Nehemiah was also *an encourager!* In chapter 3 alone, Nehemiah mentioned seventy-five people by name and, in many instances, recognized their accomplishments. He also mentioned at least fifteen *groups* of people—such as the priests, Levites, the goldsmiths, the perfumers, and the temple servants—and a number of groups from other towns and cities.

Nehemiah was definitely a "people person." He knew these individuals by name. He not only knew where they worked, but also what they had accomplished. This took time and effort. We can certainly agree that it paid rich dividends when it came to motivating these people to do their best.

Don't Miss This One

There is one very significant statement that is tucked away in this mass of data. It's easy to miss because it involves *one name* and *one word!* Nehemiah mentioned that "Baruch the son of Zabbai *zealously* repaired another section" (v. 20).

Nehemiah evidently believed this man deserved special recognition. Why? The only clue we have is that he is defined as being "zealous." Maybe he worked overtime—for nothing. Maybe he worked faster and harder. Perhaps he bypassed some of his "coffee breaks." Could it be that he worked around the clock? As stated, we really don't know why Nehemiah singled him out as being special. Whatever it was, it didn't go unnoticed by Nehemiah. He even recorded it in the eternal Word of God, and here I am writing about it thousands of years later.

My Favorite Quarterback

I remember hearing Tom Landry—longtime coach of the Dallas Cowboys—speak several years ago after his team won their first Super Bowl. He commended the whole team in various ways, but mentioned one man particularly. His name is Roger Staubach, the successful Cowboys quarterback who has become a legend in NFL history. "Roger always puts forth that extra effort," Mr. Landry said. "When the men end practice with so many required laps around the field, Roger always makes at least one more than everyone else. He's just that kind of hard-working person!" And, of course, it paid off for Roger Staubach—and the whole team.

Tom Landry let the world know that Roger Staubach put out extra effort. That's what Nehemiah did with Baruch. And don't you suppose Zabbai, his father—who was also named—beamed with pride to be identified with his son's commendation?

Becoming God's Man Today

Principles to Live By

I like the way Cyril Barber identifies the principles that made Nehemiah such a great leader.[2]

Principle 1. The Principle of Coordination

To what extent do *you* "plan your work" and then "work your plan"—and at the same time recognize God as your divine resource person?

Effective planning is absolutely essential, no matter what our vocation in life. There is no task that can be done well without careful forethought.

This principle certainly applies to every position a man can hold. But it has a particular application to husbands and fathers. A successful home results from good management. The ability to manage our homes is stated as a requirement for those who occupy leadership positions in the church (see 1 Tim. 3:4–5). This requirement also implies that God expects the church to be carefully managed. This means that elders and pastors will be good leaders if they've been good fathers.

This principle also applies to our particular positions in the business world. No one is exempt. Whether part of the management team or a member of the support staff, good planning is at the heart of every task.

Good planning begins on "paper"—but it must not remain there. It's one thing to write out goals. It's another to achieve these goals. It's one thing to have a job description; it's yet another to translate these responsibilities and ideas into action. We must both "plan our work" and "work our plan."

But we must not forget the most important factor in good leadership. Most anyone can plan—if he thinks hard enough. And most everyone can "work that plan"—if he's motivated. But a Christian—to be truly successful—must balance that effort with prayer and faith in God. Nehemiah, of course, exemplified this process.

Principle 2. The Principle of Cooperation

Again, let's focus this principle with a question. To what extent are *you* involved in your church—utilizing your talents, your gifts, your abilities, your personal resources?

The task in Jerusalem was completed because nearly everyone participated. Everyone contributed what they could. We'll see this even more clearly in the chapters that follow.

The "Body" of Christ

The Bible emphasizes the importance of total participation even more so in the New Testament than in the Old Testament. The apostle Paul emphasized this principle. He used a metaphor to get his point across—the analogy of the human body. In order for the body of Christ—the church—to grow and mature and to function properly so that it might build itself up in love, "every joint" must supply and "each individual part" *must* do its work (Eph. 4:16).

The way in which the children of Israel rebuilt the walls in Jerusalem is a beautiful illustration of what God had in mind when He designed the body of Christ—His church. Other metaphors only add to the importance of this principle of cooperation. The apostle Peter identifies the church as a "spiritual house" (1 Pet. 2:5). According to Paul, we are "God's household, having been built upon the foundation of the apostles and the prophets, Christ Jesus Himself being the cornerstone, in whom the whole building, being fitted together is growing into a holy temple in the Lord" (Eph. 2:19–21).

God's plan is clear. He wants every Christian to participate in building the church. Everyone is needed. "We, who are many, are one body in Christ, and individually members one of another" (Rom. 12:5).

Principle 3. The Principle of Commendation

To what extent are *you* an encourager—a real people person?

Over the years, I've concluded that Christians tend to neglect to encourage one another. This is tragic since we are told again and again in Scripture to encourage one another. No concept is more important than helping others to consistently do the will of God.

Remember Barnabas?

This man stands out in New Testament history as a beautiful example of a Christian who encouraged others. In fact, this is what his name means—"Son of Encouragement" (Acts 4:36). His name was changed by the apostles because this is the kind of man he was!

There are various reasons why Christians don't encourage one another. For one thing, we don't realize how important it is. If we did, we would do more of it!

Some Christians don't encourage others because they have a false view of what it will do. They're afraid it will create pride—when in actuality, encouragement helps people to overcome pride.

I've noticed that some people seemingly can't encourage others because they are so much in need of it themselves that they resort to what psychologists call "reaction formation." They sometimes become critical and discouraging. They are so preoccupied with themselves and their own weaknesses and needs that they try to tear others down to build themselves up. How sad!

A Biblical Command

Christians—of all people—should encourage one another. If we don't, we are directly disobeying specific commands of Scripture. "Therefore *encourage one another,* and build up one another," wrote Paul to the Thessalonians (1 Thess. 5:11). We also read in the Book of Hebrews—"Let us consider how to stimulate one another to love and good deeds, not forsaking our own assembling together, as is the habit of some, but *encouraging one another;* and all the more, as you see the day drawing near" (Heb. 10:24–25).

A Man Who Needed Encouragement

At one point in my vocational career, I was appointed director of the evening school at Moody Bible Institute in Chicago. When I accepted this position, I knew I faced a great challenge. No one had given specific direction to this very important work for a number of years.

The major problem I faced involved the morale of the faculty. Most of these people were members of the day school teaching team and viewed their evening school assignment as an additional burden. In some respects, this is understandable. These were evening classes, and most of the teachers were physically drained from their daytime responsibilities. Furthermore, the students who made up the evening classes were working people. After a hard day on the job, they came to school weary and tired. Though highly motivated, they sometimes found it hard to stay awake in class.

Fairly early in my directorship, I began visiting various churches in the greater Chicago area to try and meet prospective evening school students. Invariably, I would meet students who were already attending the school.

On one occasion, I remember meeting a student who voluntarily mentioned to me how much one of the professors in the evening school had meant to her. She reported that she was always tired when she arrived at school after a long day working in a downtown Chicago office. But, even though she at times struggled to stay awake during class, she made it clear that she wouldn't miss this learning experience for anything. "It's changing my life," she said.

"Aha!" I said to myself. I wrote down the student's name and the name of the professor. The next day, I called this man by phone and relayed to him exactly what the student had shared. For a moment, there was silence on the other end of the line. And then the professor responded—"Well, thanks, Gene. Thanks very, very much. I needed that!"

"Well, thank *you*, Chuck," I replied, calling him by name. "Your student, Betty, appreciates you and so do I!"

Little did I realize how much this would encourage Chuck. Sadly, I also discovered that this was the first time he had ever received this kind of positive feedback from a superior. Right there and then I determined to change all that.

I made another discovery. It didn't take long for me to realize that honest feedback like this is important and necessary. It changed a teacher's whole outlook on his task—and eventually changed the morale of the whole faculty.

Challenges from Proverbs

Sincere and honest encouragement is so easy, so inexpensive, but so powerful and motivating. Listen to this wisdom from the Book of Proverbs:

> ➤ "Anxiety in the heart of a man weighs it down, but a *good word* makes it glad" (12:25).

> ➤ *"Pleasant words* are a honeycomb, sweet to the soul and healing to the bones" (16:24).

> ➤ "Like apples of gold in settings of silver is *a word spoken in right circumstances"* (25:11).

Becoming an Effective Leader

Evaluate your life in light of Nehemiah's example as well as these New Testament correlations and applications. Ask the Holy Spirit to impress on your heart a lesson in leadership you need to apply more effectively. Then write out a specific goal. For example, you may have difficulty encouraging other people, or you may not be giving enough time to planning your work.

> ➤ I have a specific procedure for planning my work, such as:

_____ Writing out goals and standards for the month, the week, and the day

_____ Making a priority list at the beginning of each day

_____ Spending specific time doing nothing but planning

> ➤ I evaluate my effectiveness in "working my plan," by:

_____ Measuring my activities and accomplishments against my goals and standards

_____ Having others help evaluate my performance

_____ Taking special classes and refresher courses to improve my effectiveness

➤ I not only use my human resources but also draw on God's divine resources, by:

_____ Asking God for wisdom and guidance as I plan

_____ Asking God for both wisdom and strength as I work out my plans

_____ Evaluating my plans and accomplishments by means of biblical injunctions and principles

➤ I'm an active participant in the body of Christ by:

_____ Realizing I am important to other members of the Body of Christ (Rom. 12:5)

_____ Devoting myself to others in genuine brotherly love (Rom. 12:10)

_____ Honoring others above myself (Rom. 12:10)

_____ Working to produce unity in the body (Rom. 15:5)

_____ Accepting others as Christ accepted me (Rom. 15:7)

_____ Admonishing others in love (Rom. 15:14)

_____ Greeting others sincerely (Rom. 16:16)

_____ Serving others (Gal. 5:13)

_____ Carrying others' burdens (Gal. 6:2)

_____ Being tolerant toward others (Eph. 4:2)

_____ Submitting to others (Eph. 5:21)

➤ I am an "encourager" of others. This is obvious because:

_____ I tell people "thank you" when they minister to me.

_____ I give positive feedback to people when I hear others express appreciation.

_____ I tell people I'm praying for them.

_____ I ask people what prayer needs they have.

_____ I write notes of appreciation.

_____ I look for discouraged people and give them a word of encouragement.

_____ I make an effort to reach out to lonely people.

_____ I respond to others' needs with love and gentleness.

Set a Goal

With God's help, I will begin immediately to carry out the following goal in my life:

_____

_____

_____

_____

Memorize the Following Scripture

You therefore, my son, be strong in the grace that is in Christ Jesus. And the things which you have heard from me in the presence of many witnesses, these entrust to faithful men, who will be able to teach others also.
2 Tɪᴍᴏᴛʜʏ 2:1–2

Chapter 5

Overcoming Discouragement
Read Nehemiah 4:1–6

*I*n an earlier chapter, I described a miraculous answer to prayer when a group of us used Nehemiah's prayer process. We desperately needed a permanent location for our new church. However, when God enabled us to locate a piece of property on which we could construct a church building, it wasn't the "end" but just the "beginning." We faced a number of major hurdles! We had to continue to *pray diligently* and to *work hard,* and when we did, we overcame these obstacles one by one—even though there were times we wondered if we were going to succeed.

Our greatest discouragement came just as everything seemed to be in order to secure a building permit from the city of Dallas. War broke out between two major developers, and we were caught in the middle. For a time it appeared that the city council might vote to allow one of the developers to put a road right through the middle of our property. Needless to say, if this happened, it would have cratered our whole project.

The day came for a major hearing before the city council. Attorneys representing both developers argued their points. Frankly, it didn't look promising. Representing ourselves, we simply outlined our dream, our vision, our plan, and then rested our case. When the final vote was taken, our property was still intact and we had a building permit in hand.

A number of months later I was relating this story to another group of people, explaining how God had answered our prayers at that moment. After the meeting, two sympathetic Christian women approached me and informed me that they were on the city council at that time and had provided the swing vote in our favor. Once again, we saw God's sovereign will being carried out in response to our faithful efforts.

Satan Is Alive and Well

Simply reading the introductory comments in Nehemiah's journal might give the impression that once he had carefully and wisely assigned everyone to a particular section of the wall, from that point forward, everything progressed smoothly and without difficulty. Not so! From that point forward, the children of Israel faced incredible opposition from their enemies.

God's work *never* goes forward without opposition. Satan sees to that. Nehemiah's experience in rebuilding the wall of Jerusalem certainly illustrates this point graphically and dramatically.

Psychological Warfare

You'll remember that Sanballat wasn't very happy when he heard that Nehemiah was on his way "to seek the welfare of the sons of Israel" (2:10). Initially, his emotional discomfort seemed to be a minor irritation that plagues every political leader. He didn't even take Nehemiah's presence seriously. After all, what could one man do, even with the king's approval?

History was on Sanballat's side. For many years the Jews had failed to rebuild the Jerusalem wall. But Sanballat was in for a giant-sized surprise. Once Nehemiah actually arrived in Jerusalem and rallied the Jews to begin the project, Sanballat quickly saw how determined they were—and his displeasure intensified (see v. 19).

Sanballat lacked a very important factor in his historical perspective. He didn't understand God's personal interest in the children of Israel—that their failure and years in captivity related to their sin against the Lord but that their restoration related to their repentance and renewed obedience to His commands. This helps explain why Nehemiah had gained favor with King Artaxerxes. He and others in Israel who had not followed false gods had confessed Israel's sins. They prayed for forgiveness and asked God to restore them to their land (see 1:8–11). Unknown to Sanballat, that prayer was being answered and God's promises were being fulfilled.

Displeasure Turned to Anger

When Nehemiah arrived in Jerusalem and succeeded in building morale and organizing the children of Israel for the task, what was at first a minor irritation to Sanballat became a significant threat (4:1–3). His displeasure turned to anger. Nehemiah described his enemy's emotions quite graphically: "Now it came about that when Sanballat heard that we were rebuilding the wall, he became *furious and very angry*" (v. 1).

Threatened people usually react in one of three ways. Either they are extremely fearful and retreat, and you never hear from them again, or they become very angry and aggressive. To use a common expression, they are consistently "in your face"! Most often, however, they blend both fear and anger—and then attack, directly or indirectly. This was Sanballat's response. The word *furious* says it all. But it was also intense anger mixed with fear and insecurity—otherwise he would have immediately used his military power against Israel. Instead, he initially took a psychological approach.

Sanballat's Defense Mechanisms

Sanballat's initial reactions reflect his personality weaknesses—as well as the weaknesses of his associates. You don't have to be a psychologist to see this insecurity: "He spoke in the presence of his brothers and the wealthy men of Samaria and said, 'What are these feeble Jews doing? Are they going to restore it for themselves? Can they offer sacrifices? Can they finish in a day? Can they revive the stones from the dusty rubble even the burned ones?'" (4:2).

These responses reflect a very insecure man. Every question demonstrates that Sanballat was trying to convince *himself* that there was no danger. On the surface, he sounded tough and in charge. Underneath, he was worried and intensely frightened.

"The Lady Doth Protest Too Much, Me Thinks"

This common quotation from Shakespeare describes San-ballet's behavior. It's called "reaction formation." Because of deep anxiety and fear, we may reflect the opposite of what we really feel. Sanballat was not being honest with himself. If he were, he would have responded differently to what was happening in Jerusalem—even though he was intensely angry. His report before his friends may have sounded something like this:

> Nehemiah is a man to be reckoned with. He's no fool. Under his leadership, these Jews are really serious about rebuilding the walls. They're not as feeble as we think. They're actually planning to restore Jerusalem so they can live comfortably in the city and once again offer sacrifices to their God. And they're not wasting any time. They plan to complete the task as soon as possible, actually rebuilding it from dusty rubble. And with access to the king's forest, we've got a serious problem. If they accomplish this task, they'll threaten our whole economy.

Unfortunately, Sanballat's closest associate—Tobiah the Ammonite—didn't help much. He only reinforced his superior's rationalizations. Tobiah told Sanballat what he wanted to hear. With tongue-in-cheek, Tobiah retorted, "Even what they are building—if a fox should jump on it, he would break their stone wall down!" (v. 3).

"Anything You Say"

We might call Tobiah's response "identification." In order to ingratiate himself with Sanballat, he refused to be honest and allowed his leader to go on deceiving himself.

This is why mature leaders don't build around themselves "yes men"—men who are merely seeking a position of prominence and who compromise the truth in order to be accepted and promoted. Had Tobiah been mature and a true friend, he would have responded differently—perhaps as follows:

> Sanballat, I know how you feel. Your anger is understandable. I am amazed at what is happening, and I'm fearful too. But these Jews are serious. And we've got to take *them* seriously. They may appear feeble but that's because they've had no leader. They've been demoralized, but Nehemiah has changed all that. They *do* plan to restore Jerusalem and once again offer sacrifices. Maybe we'd better think twice before we fight against Israel—and their God. Don't you remember their history? They accomplished some unbelievable feats when they first settled this land. As I remember, they achieved these victories in the name of the same God that Nehemiah gives credit to for granting him favor in the eyes of King Artaxerxes.

What would have happened if Sanballat and Tobiah had responded maturely to the miracle that was taking shape before their very eyes? I believe they might have been converted to the one true God. However, they hardened their hearts and continued to deceived themselves. Consequently, they brought themselves—and many others—under a serious curse.

Spiritual Warfare

Nehemiah handled Sanballat's psychological warfare just as he had handled every other problem he had encountered thus far (vv. 4–6). He went back to basics. When he had first received the dismal report regarding the state of the Jews in Jerusalem, he immediately went to prayer (see 1:4). And now, when faced with Sanballat's demoralizing verbal attacks, he talked to God again about the matter.

Nehemiah continued utilizing this divine resource throughout the total process of rebuilding the wall. He demonstrated what Paul had in mind when he exhorted the Thessalonian Christians to "pray without ceasing" (1 Thess. 5:17).

"Aren't We to Pray for Our Enemies?"

From a Christian point of view, Nehemiah's prayer content in this situation may be difficult for us to understand—at least at first glance. He was definitely praying "against his enemies" rather than "for them." Like some of King David's imprecatory prayers, Nehemiah's prayer is also severe and condemning: "Hear, O our God, how we are despised! Return their reproach on their own heads and give them up for plunder in a land of captivity. Do not forgive their iniquity and let not their sin be blotted out before Thee, for they have demoralized the builders" (4:4–5).

How do we explain this kind of praying—especially in view of what Jesus Christ told us in the New Testament? There is an explanation.

Children of the Covenant

God had already pronounced judgment on the enemies of Israel. That's why Nehemiah could confront Sanballat so confidently earlier in our story. He told them up front that they had "no portion, right, or memorial in Jerusalem" (2:20).

God had made it clear that Jerusalem belonged to His people—the Jews—people who truly worshiped Him in spirit and in truth. But we must also remember that the same opportunity would have been given to Sanballat and others if they had responded to the truth. Sanballat was a Samaritan—a half-breed. He belonged to that group of people who had intermarried with the pagan world.

But, the Gospel Is for All

This does not mean these people were beyond redemption. Jesus demonstrated that beautifully one day while talking with *another Samaritan*—the woman at the well (see John 4:1–42). He had come into this world to save her too. Because she responded, Jesus Christ gave her "living water," which was eternal life.

The same would have happened to Sanballat and his friends. They, too, could have been saved. By responding positively to Nehemiah, they would be recognizing the Messiah that would come. However, they rejected God's grace. Consequently, God's judgment fell on them. Nehemiah then was simply praying according to God's will—that which God had already predetermined would happen to the enemies of Israel if they did not turn to the one true God (see Josh. 2:8–13).

On with the Work

Some people pray and wait for things to happen. Not Nehemiah! He prayed, and at the same time, continued to rebuild the wall (4:6). He put feet to his prayers. He faced Sanballat's psychological warfare with both spiritual and natural resources. He committed the problem to the Lord and then asked his assistants to "hand him another brick"! While praying, trusting, and working, they moved forward. Nehemiah recorded at this time that "the whole wall was joined together to half its height" (v. 6). They were halfway there. Sanballat's strategy had failed!

A Heart to Work

There's an important psychological dynamic that must not go unnoticed in this process. The children of Israel continued to make rapid progress in the midst of Sanballat's demoralizing efforts because "the people had a mind [literally a *heart*] to work" (v. 6). They did not allow discouragement—which was the focus of Sanballat's tactic—to destroy their morale.

We don't have to read between the lines to understand that Nehemiah's own enthusiasm and confidence in God served as primary factors in helping his people keep their own spirits high. This is why people need leaders who—in spite of insurmountable odds, keep right on keeping on! Tom Landry, longtime coach of the Dallas Cowboys, once said, "Leadership is a matter of having people look at you and gain confidence, seeing how you react. If you're in control, they're in control."[1]

Nothing Succeeds Like Success

At this point in time, I believe what was happening had become mutual and reciprocal. Israel's positive response to Nehemiah's leadership enabled him in turn to keep his spirits high. Once these people began to see the fruit of their efforts, they were able to encourage one another—and Nehemiah—to keep on going, in spite of Sanballat's psychological warfare.

It's at this point also that Nehemiah's integrity won the confidence of the children of Israel. They knew he was there because he cared!

Dwight Eisenhower, a great military leader, once wrote:

> In order to be a leader, a man must have followers. And to have followers, a man must have their confidence. Hence, the supreme quality for a leader is unquestionably integrity. Without it, no real success is possible, no matter whether it is on a section gang, a football field, in an army or in an office. If a man's associates find him guilty of phoniness, if they find that he lacks forthright integrity, he will fail. His teachings and actions must square with each other. The first great need, therefore, is integrity and high purpose.[2]

Becoming God's Man Today

Principles to Live By

Discouragement is one of Satan's most common methods for hindering God's work. When our morale is low, we're vulnerable and God's work will inevitably be hindered. This, of course, also includes the way we live our Christian lives.

For years, this was a problem in Jerusalem. The people of God were depressed, discouraged, and demoralized. But once they regained a proper spiritual perspective, they rose above their negative circumstances and accomplished a task that seemed impossible.

God used Nehemiah to cause this to happen. He became a dynamic leader in Israel—and his leadership formula will also work for us today, particularly when we apply His principles in the full light of New Testament teachings.

Principle 1. We should pray about situations that cause fear and anxiety.

God is interested in *every* detail of our lives—especially our moments of discouragement and disappointment. Again, we must remind ourselves of—and practice—Paul's encouraging words to the Philippians: "Be anxious for nothing, but in everything by prayer and supplication with thanksgiving let your requests be made known to God" (Phil. 4:6).

I've seen this prayer process work in my own life. Like you, I often face times when I'm anxious and frustrated. These feelings always accompany events that cause discouragement and disappointment.

Praying Specifically!

I've discovered that when I pray specifically for encouragement, God invariably answers that prayer. What intrigues me is that He usually answers that prayer by sending another Christian my way. And what often amazes me is that whatever that Christian says or does often relates specifically to the very thing that has created my discouragement. My major shortcoming is that I don't utilize this divine resource enough. But when I do, God answers prayer. This should not surprise us! It's in harmony with what God promises when we pray about anxious situations.

The "Peace of God"

After exhorting the Philippians to pray about everything—even their anxiety—Paul went on to say that "the *peace of God* which surpasses all comprehension, shall guard your hearts and your minds in Christ Jesus" (Phil. 4:7). Here Paul is not talking about "peace with God"—that divine relationship we have with the Lord because our sins are forgiven. But when he wrote to the Philippians and referred to the "peace of God," he was referring to a sense of tranquility and relaxation—an ability to overcome the anxiety that had gripped their souls.

As a Christian, are you utilizing this divine resource as you should? Remember, it's your privilege!

Principle 2. We should pray in the will of God.

To be able to pray in the will of God, we must have a good knowledge of the Word of God. It's in the Word of God that we discover the will of God.

Earlier we looked at Nehemiah's model prayer—a beautiful outline that we can use as believers today. In this chapter, we've looked at another prayer—one that uniquely relates to Nehemiah's role in coming to Jerusalem to rebuild the wall.

Why is one prayer a model and the other is not? The answer lies in understanding everything the Bible teaches us about this wonderful privilege.

Praying for Our Enemies

Let me illustrate. The New Testament never teaches us to pray down God's judgment on our enemies as Nehemiah or David did. In fact, it teaches the opposite. Is this contradictory? Not at all! It simply involves understanding the will of God and praying in accordance with His will as God has revealed that will over a process of time.

David and Nehemiah prayed in God's will as He had revealed it to them directly relative to the children of Israel and their enemies at that time. If we look at the totality of God's revelation, we can understand why it was appropriate for them and not appropriate for us.

Jesus Christ made His will very clear for us today: "You have heard that it was said, 'You shall love your neighbor, and hate your enemy.' But I say to you, love your enemies, and pray for those who persecute you" (Matt. 5:43–44).

"Father Forgive Them"

Jesus not only taught this truth but He demonstrated and lived out this principle more than any other man who ever lived. He actually prayed for those who were mocking Him. At the same time they were nailing Him to the cross, He prayed, "Father forgive them; for they do not know what they are doing" (Luke 23:34).

"Never Take Your Own Revenge"

The apostle Paul underscored the same truth. Listen to what he wrote to the Romans:

> If possible, so far as it depends on you, be at peace with all men. Never take your own revenge, beloved, but leave room for the wrath of God, for it is written, "Vengeance is Mine, I will repay, says the Lord. But if your enemy is hungry, feed him, and if he is thirsty, give him a drink; for in so doing you will heap burning coals upon his head." Do not be overcome by evil, but overcome evil with good. (Rom. 12:18–21)

Principle 3. We should combine diligent prayer with diligent work.

We've seen this principle illustrated several times in Nehemiah's ministry. The more we study Scripture, the more we see that prayer alone is seldom God's plan for us when we face difficulties. God grants us the privilege to pray about *everything* but He also expects us to do *everything* we can to resolve our problems. Sometimes we'll need to pray before we take action. At other times, we'll need to pray while we're taking action.

When we're discouraged, there are several things we can do immediately—even while we're in the process of praying.

1. *Check your energy level both physically and emotionally.* Nothing causes discouragement and interferes with our ability to cope with problems more than just plain exhaustion. The first thing we need to do when we're discouraged is to see if we need rest and relaxation. It's amazing what a good night of sleep will do for our spiritual perspectives.

Elijah illustrates the importance of this guideline more than any Old Testament prophet. After tremendous feats of faith against the prophets of Baal, he became so discouraged and depressed he wanted to die (see 1 Kings 19:4). The first thing God did in responding to his plight was to make sure he got plenty of sleep. When he awakened, the Lord had already prepared a meal for him. And once he had eaten, he slept again. When he awakened the second time, he had another meal. And after that, we read that Elijah "went in the strength of that food forty days and forty nights" (1 Kings 19:8).

This did not solve Elijah's problem completely. However, when he was rested and nourished, he was able to cope more effectively with the challenges that lay before him. It also provided the Lord with an opportunity to deal with some of Elijah's root problems.[3]

2. *Make sure you are getting proper physical exercise.* There's a greater number of people who follow this guideline today. However, there are some Christians who do not. They drive to the store, they drive around the block, they drive to school, they drive to church—and when all is said and done, they neglect this important part of their life.

It's true that the Bible teaches us that exercising ourselves spiritually is more important than exercising ourselves physically. However, if we read the Scripture correctly, Paul is teaching that physical exercise does profit. We must make sure, however, that it doesn't take precedence over disciplining ourselves "for the purpose of godliness" (1 Tim. 4:7–8).

The other side of neglecting physical exercise is the way in which we live under intense pressure in our culture—on the job, driving on expressways, working long hours, trying to compete with the "Joneses," etc. Little physical exercise combined with a lot of intense pressure is a lethal combination which will invariably affect our physical and emotional energy levels. It's imperative that as Christians we develop some form of exercise to release emotional tension and stress. If we do not, we are much more vulnerable to stressful situations and we are less able to cope with factors that cause discouragement.

3. *Spend some time with someone who is not discouraged.* Nothing pulls me out of the doldrums faster than to spend time with someone who is happy, excited, and positive about life. Conversely, I find it emotionally devastating to spend time with a negative person when I'm feeling negative myself. In this case, two negatives definitely never make a positive.

4. *Do something for someone else.* When you're discouraged, rather than sitting around feeling sorry for yourself, look for an opportunity to do something for someone else. This helps greatly to get our minds off ourselves. It's amazing how encouraged we can become when we see we've encouraged someone else.

5. *Accomplish a task.* I sometimes get discouraged because of the volume of work I face and the demands on my time. But I've also discovered that I can often overcome that discouragement by attacking my work one task at a time. Sometimes, it only means completing a little task—and suddenly, I've gained some emotional momentum, which in turn enables me to attack larger problems and resolve them. As I complete each task, I feel more and more encouraged.

6. *Attempt to learn important personal lessons from difficult situations.* It's God's will that "all things . . . work together for good to those who love God, to those who are called according to His purpose" (Rom. 8:28). However, this doesn't happen

automatically. To experience the reality in this verse, we must look for the "good" in every situation, no matter how difficult it is.

I'm reminded of Dr. Viktor Frankl who, as an educated Jew, faced the ravages of a Nazi concentration camp. Like others around him, he became horribly depressed and discouraged. Not only was he emotionally distraught but he was in a desperate state physically because of malnutrition. He actually felt as if he would die at any moment.

As a practicing psychiatrist before being taken captive by the Nazis, he had developed an approach to counseling called logotherapy. More specifically, he tried to help his patients see meaning in suffering.

While in the midst of his own suffering, Frankl attempted to practice this therapy in his own life. The only "meaning" he could see in what was happening to him was that some day he might live to tell others that his therapy worked. When he came to the place where he could hardly put one foot ahead of the other, he pictured in his mind a future day when he would be lecturing to a group of people on the subject of logotherapy—telling them how he survived those horrible experiences. By seeing this meaning in his experience, he was literally able to gain sufficient strength physically and emotionally to live to tell that story to thousands of people.

What makes this story so meaningful to me is that my wife and I actually heard Dr. Frankl share this experience one evening in a special lectureship at the University of Dallas. We had become the audience he had envisioned in his mind. We were listening to him tell how he had made his therapy work in such a desperate situation.

If this process worked for a man who at the time did not claim to be a Christian, how much more should it work for a true believer! What meaning can you see in your moment of discouragement? Is God preparing you to help someone else? Is He equipping you for greater responsibility? Will this make you a better parent, a more sensitive pastor, a more caring friend? By seeing meaning in difficult situations, we can become more mature Christians and often rise above the negative emotions we're feeling.

Becoming a Man Who Overcomes Discouragement

Reflect on the following principles and guidelines. Pray and ask the Holy Spirit to impress on your heart at least one lesson you need to apply more effectively in order to overcome discouragement. Then write out a specific goal. For example, you may not have a regular exercise program and you know you should!

> ➤ We should pray about situations that cause fear and anxiety.
> ➤ We should pray in the will of God.
> ➤ We should combine diligent prayer with diligent work.

1. Check your personal and physical energy level.
2. Make sure you are getting proper physical exercise.
3. Spend some time with someone who is not discouraged.
4. Do something for someone else.
5. Accomplish a task.
6. Attempt to learn important personal lessons from difficult situations.

Set a Goal

With God's help, I will begin immediately to carry out the following goal in my life:

_____

_____

_____

_____

Memorize the Following Scripture

And we know that God causes all things to work together for good to those who love God, to those who are called according to His purpose.
ROMANS 8:28

Chapter 6

Handling a Conspiracy
Read Nehemiah 4:7–15

Conspiracies come in all shapes and sizes. Some are as simple as several people banning together to hurt someone's feelings—worse yet, their reputation. Some are so evil that they involve a plot to harm someone physically—even committing murder.

Most of us will never forget the plot against Nancy Kerrigan during the tryouts for the 1994 Winter Olympics—an attempt by an opponent to injure her so she couldn't compete. In this case, the plan backfired—and that's exactly what happened to the men who "conspired together to come and fight against Jerusalem" (4:8).

Sanballat's Failure

As we've seen, Sanballat's psychological warfare failed. Though he succeeded in rallying Tobiah the Ammonite and Geshem the Arab to join him in order to "mock" and "despise" the Jews (2:19; 4:1), they were unable to keep the children of Israel from continuing their building project. Under Nehemiah's dynamic leadership, they had "a mind [or 'heart'] to work" and were able to complete half the task in a surprisingly short period of time (4:6).

We're not told exactly how much time had elapsed at this point, but we know that the wall was completed in an incredible fifty-two days (see 6:15). Assuming they had reached this halfway point approximately in the middle of the fifty-two-day time period, they would have been at the job only about a month. No wonder Sanballat was threatened!

What was happening in Jerusalem demonstrates another powerful ingredient in God's scheme of things. These Jews were highly motivated! They had one primary focus: to complete this task.

The Power of Unity

But there's another factor inherent in Nehemiah's comment that they "had a mind to work." Not only were they energized and excited about what they were doing, but they were literally attacking this project with a spirit of unity and oneness. They were all moving in the same direction.

It's amazing what can happen when people work together as one basic unit. What we see is Nehemiah's ingenious plan at work! This is another Old Testament picture of the way God intended the church to function (see Eph. 4:16). I'm reminded of the Jerusalem Christians centuries later when they "were of one heart and soul" (Acts 4:32).

A Universal Principle

Have you ever watched a football game where every team member seemed to be functioning at peak capacity—both on the offensive and defensive units? When this happens, a team is virtually unstoppable. It's as if they're functioning as one rather than as eleven men on the field. It's an incredible feeling—and everyone senses it!

If this can happen in a purely human endeavor, think of what can happen when God's people utilize not only their human capacities and talents but also draw on the power and wisdom of God.

This is what was happening in Jerusalem! Sanballat and all the enemies of Israel sensed it, felt it, and saw the results. Again, no wonder they were threatened. Their initial plan to demoralize the Jews had failed. They were faced with a difficult decision—either to back off and accept the fact that Israel was going to succeed, or to attack militarily.

A New Battle Plan

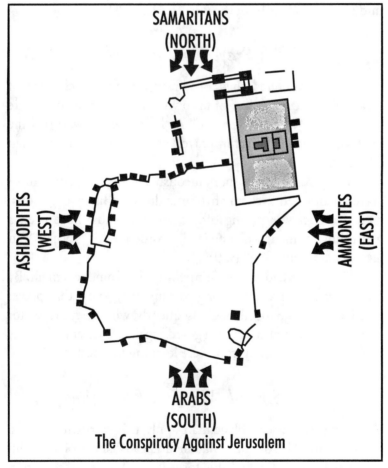

The Conspiracy Against Jerusalem

Figure 6-1

Sanballat and his cohorts were not about to back off! When they heard "that the repair of the walls of Jerusalem went on, and that the breaches began to be closed" (Neh. 4:7), they knew they needed to take more desperate measures if they were going to stop the Jews from completing the job. They called an emergency meeting and quickly concluded that they would have to launch a military attack on Jerusalem from all sides (v. 8). Sanballat and the Samaritans would attack from the north, Tobiah and the Ammonites from the east, Geshem and the Arabs from the south, and the Ashdodites from the west (see fig. 6-1).

"We Prayed to Our God"

Nehemiah countered this conspiracy against the children of Israel with a "conspiracy" of his own. They met this "corporate threat" with "corporate prayer"! As far as we know, this is the first time the burden for prayer was sensed by more than Nehemiah.

Seeing this happen spontaneously among his people must have encouraged Nehemiah tremendously. His own personal prayer model was paying off. It certainly must have been a rewarding moment when he later recorded in his journal, "But *we* prayed to our God" (v. 9)!

The people had learned something else from Nehemiah. By simply watching and listening to him, they knew that prayer and hard work go together. Consequently, while they prayed for divine help, they also "set up a guard" against their enemies "day and night" (v. 9). They, too, were learning balance!

The Struggle Was Just Beginning

All along, we've seen Nehemiah apply this spiritual formula. "Prayer" and "hard work" marched ahead hand in hand. But when the people applied this formula to this new threat from their enemies, it didn't work automatically. In fact, they faced a whole new set of problems—something they had not anticipated (see vv. 10–12).

Intense Fatigue

For at least a month, the Jews had been exerting all the energy they could muster. In spite of their superhuman success, Sanballat's psychological warfare had taken its toll. Now they faced the threat of a military attack. They not only had to work all day, but some of them had to stand guard all night. They had no fresh recruits, no "coffee breaks," and no "long weekends" or "days off." Their work—should we say—was "wall to wall"! Physical and psychological fatigue was predictable!

Double Duty

Nehemiah not only faced the problems of discouragement and fatigue among the people, but he had to add to their burdens. He needed some of them to do double duty. Since he had to assign people to stand guard, he had to reduce the number of people who could work on the wall. The work crew was reduced even further when some of them had to guard all night.

It's certainly understandable why the children of Israel began to lose their physical and emotional momentum. Looking back on what had happened, Nehemiah recorded the following interesting fact in his journal: "Thus in Judah it was said, 'The strength of the burden bearers is failing, yet there is much rubbish; and we ourselves are unable to rebuild the wall'" (v. 10).

The Problem of Paranoia

Predictably, the task before the children of Israel began to look bigger than it really was. This always happens when fatigue takes over. In this instance, little piles of dirt began to look like mountains. Even though they were half finished, the second part looked much more difficult than the first. Against this backdrop, we can understand why they were ready to give up.

The Threat of Uncertainty

To complicate matters, Nehemiah began to get reports from the Jews who lived outside of Jerusalem that their enemies were planning a secret attack. They kept hearing one clear and consistent message: "They will not know or see until we come among them, kill them, and put a stop to the work" (v. 11).

Nehemiah knew these reports were not idle gossip. He received the same message on ten different occasions—probably from different sources—but each time the message was basically the same: "They will come up against us from every place where you may turn" (v. 12). It didn't take a military genius to figure out what their enemies were planning.

The Pressure Mounts

Again, imagine what's happening in Jerusalem. The children of Israel had completed half the project, but their "emotional foundations" were crumbling. The task seemed impossible *before* they began, and now it appeared hopeless!

To add to their frustration, some of the people who lived outside of Jerusalem would naturally avoid coming into the city to work. They feared leaving their families and they didn't want to take a chance on being attacked and killed. This reduced the work force even further. From a human viewpoint, everything *would* appear hopeless! How could they possibly survive!

"Living Together" or "Dying Together"

As morale continued to sink lower with each negative report, Nehemiah knew he had to take action. Time was of the essence. As John Gardner once said—"A prime function of a leader is to keep hope alive!" This was Nehemiah's greatest challenge at that moment. He did what he knew he had to do. He "stationed men in the lowest parts of the space behind the wall, the exposed places, and [he] stationed the people in families with their swords, spears, and bows" (v. 13).

This must have been a terribly difficult decision. To place whole families together—including women and children—put tremendous pressure on everyone, fathers particularly. In case of an outright attack, they would have no choice but to stay and fight with their family members. This meant living together and/or dying together. Tough as it was, Nehemiah knew it was the only decision he could make if they were to survive—let alone succeed in rebuilding the walls. When he'd devised his initial plan, he factored this possibility into his strategy—no doubt hoping it would never materialize. But it did, and fortunately Nehemiah had prepared ahead of time!

Dealing with Fear

Anxiety and fear intensified in the hearts of the children of Israel. Nehemiah could see it written all over their faces (v. 14). Consequently, he gathered everyone together and charged them to face the situation courageously and to remember the One who was on their side. "Do not be afraid of them," he shouted. "Remember the Lord who is great and awesome" (v. 14).

Someone has said that "when the going gets tough, the tough get going." Nehemiah certainly modeled this in his own life. Though he must have been feeling much of the same fear, he couldn't allow a deteriorating situation to alter his objectives and his motivation. He had to hold his head high. He couldn't and wouldn't give up! He knew God had led him to Jerusalem to rebuild the wall. He wasn't about to forsake his divinely appointed task. If God could change Artaxerxes' mind and grant Nehemiah compassion before this ungodly man, He could certainly help his people ward off their enemies and enable them to finish the task.

A Time to Look Back!

There are times we need to pause and remember the past— even in the heat of the battle. We need to look back and review what

God has done for us on previous occasions when we have faced what appeared to be impossible situations. This is particularly necessary when we're in the midst of another insurmountable problem.

God Keeps His Promises

Nehemiah's approach in this current crisis was to first reflect on what God had done for him personally. He faced a serious challenge when he first received the report regarding the situation in Jerusalem. From a human point of view, there wasn't a thing he could do—except pray and prepare himself for an opportunity to ask the king for help. He acknowledged God as Lord—the covenant God of Israel. He also addressed Him as "the great and awesome God" (1:5).

"Would God Do It Again?"

Would this approach work again as Israel faced an even more serious crisis? In some respects, the problem was bigger since—from a human perspective—it seemed that all Nehemiah had prayed for and worked for was about to crumble and disintegrate. However, it was in the midst of this crisis that Nehemiah remembered God's promises once again and how He had been faithful to His Word. The challenge that now lay before Nehemiah was to help these people remember too!

"Remember the Lord"

It was at this moment that Nehemiah shouted with all the energy he could muster, "Remember the Lord who is great and awesome" (4:14). In other words, he was reminding the children of Israel that God had helped them before when all seemed hopeless and He would help them again. He was their covenant God! That's why Nehemiah had come to Jerusalem. That's why the Lord had granted him favor with Artaxerxes. And that's why the wall was already half built! Nehemiah knew that God would not forsake them now!

"We Must Fight"

Nehemiah followed his reminder of who God is with another difficult challenge. Nehemiah charged the people to "fight." He reminded them that they were not simply engaged in a battle for themselves but for others—their "brothers," their "sons," their "daughters," their "wives." They were fighting for the very places in which they lived—their own "houses."

Another Miracle

Prayer, hard work, and a reminder of who God really is turned the tide for Israel. Ironically, their enemies backed off when they discovered that Nehemiah had gained access to information regarding their secret attack. The Lord in turn used this "counter" information to frustrate their enemies. Apparently, they gave up the idea of attempting to stop the Jews with this clandestine maneuver. Otherwise, Nehemiah would not have reported that "all of us returned to the wall, each one to his work" (v. 15). This moral victory then spurred the Jews on and encouraged them to complete the task in spite of their physical and emotional exhaustion.

To God Be the Glory

Nehemiah's leadership philosophy becomes clear as we follow his great adventure in Jerusalem. He prayed, he trusted God, he strategized, he worked hard, he motivated people, he faced problems head-on!

When all was said and done, he gave God the glory for everything that happened. How apparent this is in his diary. Recording their moral victory over their enemies, he wrote, "And it happened when our enemies heard that it was known to us, and *that God had frustrated their plan,* then all of us returned to the wall, each one to his work" (v. 15).

Becoming God's Man Today

Principles to Live By

In addition to the principles we've already looked at from previous episodes in Nehemiah's life—the effectiveness of prayer, the necessity of balancing human effort with God's sovereign plans, the power of motivation and unity—there are several other very practical lessons. In fact, it's possible to get so caught up in the intense spiritual and psychological dynamics in this story, that it's easy to miss these simple but profound principles.

Principle 1. It's often more difficult to complete the second half of a task than the first half.

Once the Jews reached the halfway point in rebuilding the wall around Jerusalem, they faced a normal motivational problem. Of course, for them it was not a normal challenge. They were faced with a possibility of a military attack from all sides. However, even in the best of times, it's easy to "let down" when we're halfway there.

A Football Metaphor

The Jews were definitely ahead at halftime when they went into the locker room. Nehemiah was definitely a better quarterback. Sanballat, on the other hand, couldn't seem to get his team off the line of scrimmage.

But come the second half, things were different. Nehemiah's team had worked their hearts out. They were physically and emotionally exhausted. Sanballat, on the other hand, brought in fresh recruits and a whole new set of plays.

This analogy is appropriate for a couple of reasons. First, there's always a natural tendency for most of us to start strong as we attack a challenging project. But once we get into the thick of it, it's easy to lose momentum—particularly if we're putting out a lot of energy. Furthermore, once we get beyond the opening minutes (or hours) and settle into the step-by-step process, it's also easy to lose sight of the goal. Excitement normally wanes when we get into the steady, day-by-day, nitty-gritty responsibilities of life.

Second, it's also easy to get caught off guard when we're winning. We sometimes let our guard down. It's then that we can lose perspective and momentum. The tide can turn quickly.

Third, our tendency to "let down" is accentuated when we grow weary. In fact, even as I write this sentence I'm aware of the fact that I've worked hard on this chapter most of the day. Furthermore, I'm physically and mentally tired. If it were not for a very important deadline, I'd put a period at this point and retire!

It takes unusual motivation to complete difficult tasks when we're tired. Some people are surprised when I tell them that completing writing projects is a difficult task for me. Though I have written a number of books, I always have to generate a great deal of self-discipline and motivation to achieve these goals.

How many worthy projects are there in our Christian lives which we tackle enthusiastically, but never get beyond the halfway point? Remember! First, it's a natural tendency. Second, fatigue and boredom will try to stop us every time. Third, Satan delights in uncompleted tasks—particularly ones that are spiritually productive.

Principle 2. Fatigue combined with a sense of uncertainty makes it difficult for all of us to correctly evaluate reality.

What appears to be an achievable goal in the beginning stages of a project can become overwhelming and threatening when we get tired. This was part of Israel's problem. Because they ran out of steam physically, the piles of rubbish near the wall seemed to be getting larger even though they were actually getting fewer and smaller.

The Power of a Positive Attitude

Every good coach knows that a game is often won or lost on the basis of mental attitude. A team can beat itself by viewing their opponents as being bigger and better than they are. On the other hand, inferior teams have beaten stronger teams by maintaining positive mental attitudes. When a team gets tired, the other team *always* looks bigger and better—even though they may not be.

When a dose of uncertainty and insecurity are added to our fatigue, our imaginations begin to run wild. It's easy to get paranoid. Before long, we have become negative thinkers and only see the dark side of life. In a sense, this is what happened in Jerusalem. The threat of a secret attack only added fuel to their defeatist attitudes.

Has This Ever Happened to You?

I've known Christians who have gotten caught up in right-wing political and/or religious organizations that concentrate on the problems in our society. Before long, all they can think and talk about are the negative things that are happening in our lives. They become obsessed with feelings of doom and gloom. Some even live in constant anxiety—fear that they're going to lose everything they own; fear that they are going to lose their freedoms; fear that they are going to suffer both physically and psychologically at the hands of the enemies of historical American values.

Certainly, there are bad omens in our society. We are deteriorating. But on the other hand, Christians should be able to live above these circumstances. No matter what happens in our culture, we must remind ourselves that we are citizens of heaven. We have a home prepared for us that is not built with human hands. As Christians, we should be positive—not negative. This does not mean we shouldn't be realistic. But it also means we shouldn't be pessimistic. The Bible teaches that we are to be people of hope.

What a Powerful Model

If anyone could have adopted a doom-and-gloom philosophy, it was Nehemiah. But he didn't allow this to happen. He faced his problems head-on. He didn't hide his head in the sand. Neither did he allow these problems to overwhelm him, sidetrack him, and eventually defeat him and his people. Together—with the help of God—the Israelites rose above the problems of fatigue and uncertainty and succeeded in thwarting their enemies' efforts to destroy them.

Principle 3. Effective leadership involves both modeling and exhortation.

Again, Nehemiah illustrates this principle beautifully. What he *was,* the people who followed him *were becoming!* They prayed like him and they worked like him. But there also came a time when Nehemiah had to remind the people who God was, what He had done for them, and that they should trust His promises. He also had to exhort them to fight and stand firm against their enemies—no matter what the price.

All Christians need good models and proper teaching. Any good leader—whether father, mother, pastor, counselor, or teacher—knows that both are necessary. We must never neglect these qualities in helping others to discover the will of God.

Becoming a Positive Role Model

Words spoken that are not illustrated in life are often hollow and meaningless. In the words of Paul, they become like "a noisy gong or a clanging cymbal" (1 Cor. 13:1). On the other hand, words spoken against the backdrop of a good model are meaningful and difficult to ignore.

As you reflect on the following questions and suggestions, pray and ask the Holy Spirit to impress on your heart at least one lesson you need to apply more effectively in order to become a positive role model. Then write out a specific goal. For example, you may have several worthy projects that are at a standstill—they need to be completed.

_____ What worthy projects do you have in process that are only half finished and at a standstill? Which of these projects would be the most spiritually productive for other people in your life—a member of your family, a close Christian friend, or perhaps a non-Christian friend?

_____ In what area of your life do you struggle most with paranoid feelings? Could it be because of physical and emotional exhaustion? To what extent are your mental and emotional distortions related to feelings of uncertainty, inferiority, and insecurity? Can you think of other reasons? Decide now how you might rise above these problems. You might:

➤ Talk with a close friend who will listen to you and give you good advice.

➤ Talk with a competent Christian counselor.

➤ Take a good vacation.

➤ Develop more open communication with a close friend or your marital partner.

As a Christian parent, pastor, teacher, counselor, or business person, to what extent are you first and foremost a good model of Christlike behavior as well as someone who speaks openly about his faith?

Set a Goal

With God's help, I will begin immediately to carry out the following goal in my life:

_____

_____

_____

_____

Memorize the Following Scripture

Now for this very reason also, applying all diligence, in your faith supply moral excellence, and in your moral excellence, knowledge; and in your knowledge, self-control, and in your self-control, perseverance, and in your perseverance, godliness; and in your godliness, brotherly kindness, and in your brotherly kindness, Christian love.

2 PETER 1:5–7

Chapter 7
___

An Incredible Fifty-two Days
Read Nehemiah 4:15–23

*M*ention the name Dr. Henrietta Mears and many people today wouldn't have a clue who you're talking about. However, in my mind, she's one of the great Christians of our century. God used her greatly. Campus Crusade for Christ was launched out of her home next to the UCLA campus. She had a direct influence on Bill Bright, who founded this great ministry. Billy Graham wrote in the introduction to her biography that no woman other than his mother had a greater influence in his life.

For years, she taught a Sunday School class at the Hollywood Presbyterian Church that touched the lives of thousands of young people. At least six hundred young men went into the ministry as a result of her influence. At one point in time, it was said that she had led more people to Christ on the West Coast than any other person.

My wife and I had the privilege of knowing Dr. Mears personally. To be with her was an inspiring experience. Her enthusiasm was contagious! She was the first person who called my attention to the fact that the word *enthusiastic* comes from the basic word meaning "God in us"! I'll never forget that insight—primarily because Henrietta Mears not only used the word "enthusiastically" but gave new meaning to the concept by the way she lived.

And yet, the thought I remember most is the answer she gave to a question as she entered the golden years of her life. "Dr. Mears," someone asked, "if you could live your life all over again, what would you do differently?" Without a moment's hesitation, she responded, "I'd simply believe God more!"

When I think of this comment by Dr. Mears, I can't help but think of Nehemiah. He was a great man of faith. Yet, if he were to live his life over again, he'd probably respond with the same words—"I'd simply believe God more!"

Nehemiah's Strategy Worked

When Sanballat and his cohorts discovered that their plan for a secret attack on Jerusalem was common knowledge and that Israel had organized to defend themselves, they backed off! When this happened, the children of Israel developed renewed courage. In spite of their fatigue, their fears, and their limited resources, they continued to rebuild the walls.

At the same time, Nehemiah took no chances. Though he knew God was unquestionably on their side (see 4:15), he never presumed on God's supernatural care. He beefed up his efforts at being prepared for a surprise attack. He was wise enough to know that the information that was being passed along could also be propaganda.

"From That Day On"

From that day on, half of Nehemiah's servants "carried on the work while half of them held the spears, the shields, the bows, and the breastplates" (v. 16). Even those who continued the work carried weapons. Some transported material, but used one hand while they carried a weapon in the other (see v. 17). The rest of the work force who actually built the walls used both hands—but each carried a weapon at his side (see v. 18).

Nehemiah took another precaution. He knew they were all vulnerable because the workers were doing their jobs all around the wall. Consequently, Nehemiah stationed a trumpeter next to him. As he moved from place to place supervising the work, the trumpeter followed him. If there were an attack, he would blow the trumpet and everyone was to come to one central location to brace themselves for a counterattack.

"Our God Will Fight for Us"

To make sure the people really knew why they could proceed with confidence, Nehemiah once again underscored the divine nature of their task. In the same breath that he issued a warning to listen to the trumpet blast so they could prepare for military action, he also said, "Our God will fight for us" (v. 20). In other words, Nehemiah was once again telling the children of Israel that if they did their part—including moving ahead by faith—God would do His part.

The work went forward! Everyone worked diligently—from the crack of "dawn until the stars appeared" (v. 21). Those living outside the city didn't even return to their homes. Rather, they spent the night in Jerusalem, laboring by day and guarding by night. And even when they stopped to rest, they didn't remove their clothes. They kept their weapons within arm's reach so that at a moment's notice they could be ready to defend themselves (see v. 23).[1]

"With the Help of Our God"

Against insurmountable odds, the children of Israel actually completed the wall in an incredible fifty-two days (see v. 15). This was an amazing feat. In fact, when Israel's enemies saw what had happened, "they lost their confidence" (v. 16). They recognized that they had just witnessed a supernatural event—namely, that the children of Israel had completed this project with God's help (see v. 16).

When Nehemiah had first rallied the people to begin rebuilding the wall, Sanballat, Tobiah, and Geshem had mocked Nehemiah when he told the people that "the God of heaven" would enable them to complete this project (2:20). Obviously, Nehemiah's words fell on deaf ears! These pagan men didn't believe it was possible, even from a human point of view. But now—fifty-two days later—they looked on in utter amazement. Hopefully, Nehemiah's earlier words were running through their minds—and ringing loudly in their ears. At least, they now understood what Nehemiah had said.

Charles Swindoll, writing about this grand culmination, states: "That has to be the most thrilling experience in the world—to watch God come to the rescue when you have been helpless. In the middle of the incessant assault of the enemy, in spite of the endless verbal barrage, the wall was built! While the enemy blasts, God builds."[2]

Becoming God's Man Today

Principles to Live By

What can we learn from Nehemiah's experience as he led the children of Israel to complete this task in the midst of such great opposition?

Principle 1. We must be on constant guard against our greatest enemy.

Most of our battles as Christians are on a much different level than the people of God in the Old Testament. In fact, God has never called us to defend our faith with literal weapons. We cannot justify a holy war on the basis of God's plans for Israel. "Our struggle," Paul wrote to the Ephesians, "*is not against flesh and blood,* but against the rulers, against the powers, against the world forces of this darkness, against *the spiritual forces of wickedness* in the heavenly places" (Eph. 6:12).

In this New Testament passage, Paul drew both a unique parallel and a distinction between a "flesh and blood" battle, and our "spiritual" battles. Referring to various pieces of armor and weapons used by ancient warriors, Paul made a direct application to the Christian's battle against Satan and his host of demons: "Put on the full armor of God, that you may be able to stand firm against the schemes of the devil" (6:11).

What are these weapons and what are the devil's schemes? Paul answered both of these questions clearly in this Ephesian passage.

First, gird "your loins with truth" (Eph. 6:14). God is the author of truth. Conversely, Satan is the "father of lies" (John 8:44). Jesus Christ, God's Son, is the perfect embodiment of truth, for He said, "I am the . . . truth" (John 14:6).

There is no scheme so subtle as false information. Not surprising, Satan uses it constantly against Christians. It's demoralizing and destructive. He uses lies to destroy marriages, families, and the church. And, of course, when he scores a victory in any one of these areas, he has hurt our Christian witness in the world.

We must remember that a lie was Satan's first evil tactic that plunged the whole world into sin. When Satan first approached Eve in the garden of Eden, he tempted her to eat of the fruit of the tree in the midst of the garden—something God said she should not do lest she die. "You surely shall not die," Satan told her—which was the very opposite of what God had said (Gen. 2:17; 3:4).

Sadly, Eve believed Satan rather than God. Adam was deceived also, and together this couple introduced sin into their lives and into the lives of everyone born thereafter—including all of us living today (see Rom. 5:12).

From that moment forward, we have all found it easy to believe lies—and sometimes to tell them—particularly about other people. We also have found it easy to deceive ourselves. Consequently, Paul wrote, "Stand firm therefore, having girded your loins with truth" (Eph. 6:14). This is a powerful weapon against Satan.

Second, "put on the breastplate of righteousness" (Eph. 6:14). Not only is Satan the father of lies, but he's the author of all wickedness and evil in the world. One of His greatest goals is to cause Christians to live unholy lives. He's been hard at work at this task ever since sin first entered the world.

Have you ever noticed how much easier it is to gravitate toward sin than righteousness; toward immorality than morality; to be attracted to unholy behavior rather than holy behavior; to participate in ungodliness rather than godliness? This natural tendency in itself affirms the fact that the principle of sin is at work in our lives.

Remember, too, that when we do sin, we find it easier to commit another sin. When this happens, it's easy to get caught up in a web of unrighteousness. The good news is that this does not need to happen. We have the secret to overcoming Satan. That's why Paul exhorts us always to have the "breastplate of righteousness" in place. Satan's darts cannot penetrate this piece of armor (Eph. 6:14).

Third, "shod your feet with the preparation of the gospel of peace" (Eph. 6:15). There's some question as to what Paul means by this piece of armor. Personally, I believe it has to do with the good news of salvation in Jesus Christ. Remember Paul's words to the Romans? He stated that "we have *peace with God* through our Lord Jesus Christ." This is what happens when we've been "justified by faith" (Rom. 5:1).

This is the good news for all of us who have put our faith in Jesus Christ. In Christ, we have "peace with God"—and there's no greater defense against Satan than this great eternal truth.

Look back at the opening part of Paul's letter to the Ephesians. You'll discover that he laid the groundwork for what he would later share in this passage in which he outlines God's armor. Speaking of their preconversion state, Paul reminded them that they had "no hope" and were "without God in the world" (2:12). But that was no longer true. They had "been brought near by the blood of Christ. For, *He Himself is our peace,*" wrote Paul (vv. 13–14).

Could it be that Paul was referring back to the fact that Jesus Christ is "our peace" when he exhorted these believers to prepare their feet with "the *gospel of peace*" (6:15)? Personally, I think this is what Paul had in mind.

Fourth, take "up the shield of faith" (Eph. 6:16). It's true that as Christians we're saved by faith (see Eph. 2:8–9). However, once we have put our faith in Christ for salvation, we must then *walk by faith* (see Col. 2:6). It's this piece of armor, Paul wrote, with which we "will be able to extinguish all the flaming missiles of the evil one" (Eph. 6:16).

This is what we see illustrated in Hebrews chapter 11. There we meet a number of Old Testament greats who conquered their enemies by faith. Though many of their victories involved literal battles, they also had many victories that were spiritual. In this sense, they become a "cloud of witnesses" that we can look to for strength and encouragement. Consequently, we read—"Let us also lay aside every encumbrance, and the sin which so easily entangles us, and let us run with endurance the race that is set before us, fixing our eyes on Jesus *the author and perfecter of faith*" (Heb. 12:1–2).

No matter what happens to us as Christians, we must continue to believe God—to believe that He loves us, that He cares for us, that He wants to help us.

Many years ago, John Yates captured the meaning of Paul's words in his lyrics, which were later set to music by Ira Sankey.[3]

> Encamped along the hills of light,
> Ye Christian soldiers, rise,
> And press the battle ere the night
> Shall veil the glowing skies;
> Against the foe in vales below
> Let all our strength be hurled;
> Faith is the victory, we know,
> That overcomes the world.

Fifth, "take the helmet of salvation" (Eph. 6:17). Satan is called the "accuser of [the] brethren" (Rev. 12:10). He delights in creating insecurity and fear, particularly regarding our personal relationship with Jesus Christ.

When I became a Christian, my first temptation was to doubt my salvation. For several years I fought a tremendous spiritual battle. When I felt good, I felt saved; when I felt bad, I felt lost. My security was based on my feelings—not on the truth of the Word of God.

Satan generated these doubts because I did not understand the gospel of Christ in its fullness. I didn't understand my security in Jesus Christ—that nothing can separate me from His love (see Rom. 8:35–39). Once I understood this truth and believed it, I had peace in my heart. Even when I felt down, I still knew that God was the unchangeable One. His promises were true. He would never go back on His word. To stand effectively against Satan, I had to learn to "take the helmet of salvation." I had been "sealed with [the] Holy Spirit of promise." He has guaranteed my "inheritance until the redemption of the purchased possession" (Eph. 1:13–14, KJV). Thank God, I am that "purchased possession"—and so are you if you have received Christ as your personal Savior!

Sixth, "take . . . the sword of the Spirit, which is the word of God" (Eph. 6:17). At this point when describing the armor of God, Paul became very specific. Our greatest defense against Satan is the Bible. Scripture even describes our enemy and his evil schemes in great detail. We're told exactly how to defeat him—which is graphically illustrated in this very passage.

In Ephesians chapter 6, we learn that the Word of God is "the sword of the Spirit." This is one of the main reasons God sent His Holy Spirit into the world and into the hearts of Christians. God wants to reveal Himself through the Holy Scriptures.

Jesus made this very clear to the apostles. Several times He told these men that when He returned to heaven, the heavenly Father would send "the *Spirit of truth*" to counsel them and to help them (John 14:17; 15:26; 16:13). "He will teach you all things," Jesus said, "and bring to your remembrance all that I said to you" (John 14:26).

Later, Jesus was even more specific regarding one of the Holy Spirit's primary purposes in coming into the world. Preparing them for His departure, Jesus said, "But when He, the *Spirit of truth*, comes, He will guide you into all the truth . . . and He will disclose to you what is to come" (John 16:13).

This promise began to be fulfilled on the Day of Pentecost when the Holy Spirit descended on that small band of Christians who were gathered in the Upper Room in the city of Jerusalem. When the Holy Spirit came upon them, it enabled the apostles particularly—but not exclusively—to speak forth the very words of God. This is what enabled the New Testament believers to "devote themselves to the apostles' teaching" (Acts 2:42).

Later, the apostles and several other men recorded this divine truth for us in writing—which today comprises the New Testament documents. The Holy Spirit continues to work in our hearts as He continues to speak to us through the Scriptures. Like Joshua, we're to meditate on the Scriptures and to make them a part of our lives (see Josh.1:8). As we do, we're able "to stand firm against the schemes of the devil" (Eph. 6:11) by taking "the sword of the Spirit, which is the word of God" (6:17).

Seventh, "pray at all times in the Spirit" (Eph. 6:18). As the apostle Paul culminates this paragraph, he departs from his metaphor and makes a very direct statement regarding prayer. As we've seen from our studies in Nehemiah, this has always been and always will be the Christian's greatest weapon against Satan.

Paul also emphasized consistency in prayer. "Pray at all times," he wrote. Furthermore, he wrote that we are to pray "in the Spirit"—that is, we are to pray according to the will of God.

At this point, Paul correlated prayer with his previous exhortation—to take "the sword of the Spirit, which is the word of God" (v. 17). In other words, there's only one way for us as

Christians to be sure we're praying "in the Spirit." It's to pray according to what we know God has already revealed to us—the revelation that has come from the "Spirit of truth" and which is recorded in the Holy Scriptures. Consequently, the more we know of God's Word, the more we can pray "in the Spirit," knowing with certainty that we are praying according to the will of God.

Principle 2. We must stand together in our battles against Satan.

One of the greatest challenges Nehemiah faced in rebuilding the wall was to develop a strategy so that they could stand together in case of attack. "The work is great and extensive," he said, "and we are separated on the wall far from one another" (Neh. 4:19). As we've seen, he appointed a man who would follow him everywhere he went, and in case of attack, he was to "sound the trumpet." At that point, everyone was to rally to that spot (see 4:20).

Just so, God never intended for Christians to face Satan and his host of demons alone. We need each other. There is strength in unity and mutual support and encouragement. This is why Jesus prayed for unity among Christians (John 17:21, 23). And this is why Paul exhorted all of us to make every effort to "preserve the unity of the Spirit in the bond of peace" (Eph. 4:3).

Satan's greatest target is the church of Jesus Christ. Whether we are individuals, marital partners, families, or local bodies of believers, Satan desires to "break down our walls"! Following through on this Old Testament metaphor, Satan doesn't even want us to continue the building process. But what we've just looked at is a very specific "battle plan" for defeating our greatest enemy. We have God's assurance that we can overcome Satan victoriously in this building venture. Paul made this clear with another metaphor—also written to the Ephesians:

> So then you are no longer strangers and aliens, but you are fellow-citizens with the saints, and are of God's household, having

been built upon the *foundation* of the apostles and prophets, Christ Jesus Himself being the *corner stone*, in whom the *whole building*, being fitted together is growing into a holy temple in the Lord; in whom you also are being built together into a dwelling of God in the Spirit. (Eph. 2:19–22)

We're all more vulnerable when we try to live the Christian life in isolation. I know this is true in my own life. When I am out of harmony with other Christians—my wife, my children, or any of my brothers or sisters in Christ—I am far more vulnerable to Satan's attacks.

This is addressed in the passage in Ephesians. Unfortunately, we often approach these instructions and think of them as merely applicable to our personal lives. Though each of us as a Christian must certainly put on God's armor, the basic meaning of this passage is that we as believers are to wage war on Satan as a group.

As a body of believers, we are to "be strong in the Lord" (Eph. 6:10). As a church, we are to "put on the full armor of God" so that we may be able to "stand firm against the schemes of the devil" (v. 11). Practically speaking, this means we're to look out for one another. We are to protect one another; we are to "lay down our lives" for one another (1 John 3:16). This is the secret to victory against Satan and his evil forces.

Principle 3. We should say with Nehemiah, "Our God will fight for us" (4:20).

As we've seen throughout this study thus far, all of us as human beings are responsible to respond to God's will. *We* must follow God's instructions. *We* must obey His commands. *We* must do His will. But ultimately, God is the One who wins the victory—just as we've seen in every lesson that has emerged from our study of Nehemiah.

Paul made this clear in his Letter to the Ephesians. Though we are responsible to "put on the whole of armor of God," we are also to "be strong in the Lord, and in the strength of His might" (Eph. 6:10).

Balancing our human responsibility with our reliance on God will always be a struggle for each of us in our war against Satan. Unfortunately, we tend to avail ourselves of God's divine resources only when we seemingly can't handle the problems of life in our own strength. In this sense, our Christianity often becomes more of a convenience that we use only to meet our own needs. When Christ puts demands on our lives that we don't like, we find it easy to turn away from Him and take matters into our own hands.

Have You Met Kefa?

One day at the Christian Booksellers Association, my wife and I had the privilege of meeting an African pastor who marked our lives in a unique way. If you've read any of my previous books, you've met him before. His name is F. Kefa Sempangi. Kefa wrote a book entitled *A Distant Grief,* which was the story behind the martyrdom of Christians in Uganda during Idi Amin's evil reign.

Kefa's experience marked our lives. As we listened to him tell his story, the pain was so deep that we shed tears. Our response was not so much related to the horrible experiences faced by these Christians which often resulted in excruciating pain and death, but rather, the way in which their commitment revealed our own apathy as Christians.

Kefa miraculously escaped from Uganda and came to the United States. He had opportunity to study in a seminary in the East. He shared the changes that quickly took place in his life. The greatest change he said came in his prayer life. Here's what he had to say:

> In Uganda I had prayed with a deep sense of urgency. I refused to leave my knees until I was certain I had been in the presence of the resurrected Christ. It was not just the gift I needed. I needed to see the Giver. I needed to know that the God of orphans and widows, the God of the helpless, heard my prayers. Now, after a

year in Philadelphia, the urgency was gone. When I prayed publicly I was more concerned to be theologically correct than to be in God's presence. Even in private my prayers were no longer the helpless cries of a child. They were spiritual tranquilizers, thoughts that made no contact with anything outside themselves. More and more, I found myself coming to God with vague requests for gifts I did not expect.

One night, I said my prayers in a routine fashion and was about to rise from my knees when I heard the convicting voice of the Holy Spirit.

"Kefa, who were you praying for? What is it you wanted? I used to hear the names of children in your prayers, the names of friends and relatives. You prayed for Okelo and Topista, for Dr. K. and Ali, for Nakazi and your father. Now you pray for 'the orphans,' for 'the church' and your 'fellow refugees.' Which refugees, Kefa? Which believers? Which orphans? Who are these people and what is it you want for them?"

It was a sharp rebuke. As I fell again to my knees and asked for forgiveness for my sin of unbelief, I knew that it was not just my prayers that had suffered. It was not just a bad memory that caused names to vanish from my mind and turned those closest to me into abstractions. God Himself had become a distant figure. He had become a subject of debate, an abstract category. I no longer prayed to Him as a living Father but as an impersonal being who did not mind my inattention and unbelief.

From that night on, my prayers became specific. I prayed for real people, with real needs. And it was not long before, once again, these needs became the means by which I came face to face with the living God. [4]

Are You a "Mechanical Soldier"?

One of my favorite ballets is "The Nutcracker." In her dream, a little girl sees a toy soldier come to life. He struts about in mechanical fashion carrying out his duties. He's fun to watch—but, of course, it's all a dream!

As I reflect on my own Christian life, I am sometimes reminded of this "toy soldier." It's easy to perform "mechanically" and "routinely"—thinking I'm living for Christ and waging battle against Satan. But in reality, I'm simply "playing a game." What about you? Are there times when you can also identify?

In our own comfortable environment, it's easy to be lulled to sleep because of our blessings and our freedoms. If we're not careful, we can operate like mechanical Christians—without hearts of compassion and without a sense of urgency. If Kefa found it easy to be lulled into a state of complacency in only one year—after experiencing years of persecution and attacks on his own life—how easy it is for us to be lulled into an even greater state of complacency. Sadly, we don't even know we're complacent since we don't have a backdrop of persecution to evaluate our attitudes and actions.

Don't Misunderstand

I don't believe we should feel badly because God has blessed us! However, I believe we ought to feel ashamed if we're not thankful—if we're not grateful—if we're selfish and unwilling to share with others. I believe we ought to feel badly if we are only academic followers of Jesus Christ. If we have been lulled into a state of complacency, then Satan has already won the battle in our lives. We've been defeated and we may not even know it.

Becoming a Man Who Defeats Satan

The Scriptures are clear. God wants us to be Christians who see beyond our affluence, our luxuries, and our freedoms to see a God who cares for us and others. He wants us to see Himself—a God who wants to fight for us and help us not to become enmeshed in a materialistic and immoral world that can dull our sensitivities to His Word and the things of the Spirit. He wants us to be victorious over Satan!

➤ We must be on constant guard against our greatest enemy.

➤ We must stand together in our battles against Satan.

➤ We should say, just as Nehemiah said, "Our God will fight for us!"

As you reflect on these principles and the following questions, pray and ask the Holy Spirit to impress on your heart at least one lesson you need to apply more effectively in order to overcome Satan. Then write out a specific goal. For example, you may find it easy to distort the truth. Or you may have discovered you're living more of a "man-centered" life than a "God-centered life."

1. To what extent am I constantly standing guard against Satan's subtle attacks on my life? What is my greatest need based on the following checklist:

_____ a. I need to gird my loins with truth.

_____ b. I need to put on the breastplate of righteousness.

_____ c. I need to shod my feet with the preparation of the gospel of peace.

_____ d. I need to take the shield of faith.

_____ e. I need to put on the helmet of salvation.

_____ f. I need to take the sword of the Spirit which is the Word of God.

_____ g. I need to pray at all times in the Spirit.

2. To what extent am I making every effort to maintain the unity of the Spirit in the bond of peace? What am I doing that contributes to disunity rather than unity?

3. To what extent is my Christian life "man-centered" rather than "God-centered"? Am I trying to operate in my own strength rather than in the strength of the Lord?

Set a Goal

With God's help, I will begin immediately to carry out the following goal in my life:

Memorize the Following Scripture

> *Finally, be strong in the Lord, and in the strength of His might. Put on the full armor of God, that you may be able to stand firm against the schemes of the devil. For our struggle is not against flesh and blood, but against the rulers, against the powers, against the world forces of this darkness, against the spiritual forces of wickedness in the heavenly places.*
> EPHESIANS 6:10–12

Chapter 8
<u></u>

Conflict Resolution
Read Nehemiah 5:1–13

*A*nyone who has been in a leadership position has had to wrestle with conflict resolution. Whether CEO, president, pastor, father, or husband—wherever you have two or more people—disagreements are inevitable. Some conflicts are easy to resolve. Others are complex and terribly time consuming. Unfortunately, some are unsolvable.

One thing is certain. If at all possible, conflicts must be resolved. If they're not, organizational efficiency and productivity can drop to zero. Churches will split, families are left in a chaotic state, and marriages blow apart!

An Intense Internal Problem

In the midst of Nehemiah's incredible challenge to defeat his enemies and at the same time to keep rebuilding the wall, he was hit with an internal problem that is almost unimaginable. Most of us have never faced a conflict so great and so demanding—and hopefully never will. In this instance, the timing could not have been worse!

But as with all internal conflicts, they *must* be resolved—and as soon as possible. If they're not, they'll get worse. In Israel's case, if Nehemiah had not faced this problem head-on, it could have scuttled the whole building project and would have spelled victory for Israel's enemies. Worse yet, it would have brought reproach on the name of the Lord!

"There Was a Great Outcry"

The conflict Nehemiah faced in Israel was so severe that "there was a great outcry of the people and of their wives against their Jewish brothers" (5:1). This was no minor problem! It was complex—and had been brewing for a long time.

First, some were running out of food. "We, our sons and our daughters, are many," they complained; "therefore let us get grain that we may eat and live" (v. 2).

Second, many who had enough to eat were putting food on their tables by mortgaging their fields, their vineyards, and their homes (v. 3).

Third, others—in order to keep their property—were borrowing money from their Jewish brothers to pay taxes to King Artaxerxes (see v. 4). The problem was compounded when those who borrowed money were charged exorbitant interest rates by their own Jewish brothers.

Fourth—and the worst of all—when their crops failed, their creditors took away their property and sold their children into slavery (see v. 5). These people were left in a hopeless state. There was no way out. "We are helpless," they cried out to Nehemiah, "because our fields and vineyards belong to others" (v. 5).

How Could This Be?

There are some logical—but inexcusable—reasons why these conflicts existed. *First,* many in Judah had dedicated themselves to rebuilding the walls—including those with meager resources. *Second,* they were experiencing a famine (see v. 3), which complicated matters terribly. Some were not able to produce enough food to sustain themselves. At the same time, those who had plenty in Israel were taking advantage of the poor.

There was probably another reason. The small farms that belonged to the children of Israel were always considered fair game by their enemies. At times—after the farmers had waited patiently for the harvest—rebel bands descended on their fields and vineyards and stripped them clean. In view of the psychological warfare that was already being used against Israel, it doesn't take too much imagination to conclude that their enemies were also contributing to their internal problems.

Double Trouble

Imagine, if you can, what Nehemiah must have been feeling when he faced these new problems. He had already been waging a psychological battle against Israel's enemies. He felt the full weight of the responsibilities to keep Israel in a state of military emergency and, at the same time, to keep building the wall! And now this!

There are times when a leader wants to give up. The pressures are so great it seems impossible to go on. I am confident Nehemiah must have had these feelings. Frankly, I've had them with far less pressure.

But again, "when the going gets tough, the tough get going"! This is exactly what happened to Nehemiah. Again, we see the power in his personality. He had come too far to give up now!

"The Straw That Broke the Camel's Back"

When everyone else in Israel had been ready to give up the ship, Nehemiah had stood firm against impossible odds—exhorting his people to trust God and not to give up. When morale had hit rock bottom, he didn't dare show signs of personal fatigue and discouragement.

But now, internal strife? It was the "straw that broke the camel's back"! Fathers and mothers and children were going hungry. Families were losing their properties and sources of income. Sons and daughters were being sold into slavery. And worst of all, brothers were taking advantage of brothers in the midst of this crisis situation! It was too much! "Then I was *very angry*," reports Nehemiah, "when I had heard their outcry and these words" (v. 6).

Righteous Anger

Nehemiah's emotions were prompted by more than low physical and psychological tolerance. Though it's logical and understandable that this must have been a factor, it was not the primary reason. His anger was directed at selfishness, greed, and insensitivity. People were hurting and suffering—and those who should have been the most compassionate were the most guilty of exploitation.

"I Consulted with Myself"

At this point, we can discover one of the most important lessons we'll ever learn from Nehemiah's experience. In spite of his intense anger, he did not take immediate action. Rather, he backed off, got control of himself, and did some very careful and serious thinking. Nehemiah described it this way: "I consulted with myself" (v. 7).

The Hebrew word translated *consult* literally means "to give oneself advice" or to "counsel oneself." In order to get at all the facts, Nehemiah got distance on the problem. This in itself enabled him to cool down. He got proper perspective on the total problem before deciding what to do.

What Does God Have to Say?

As a spiritual leader, Nehemiah knew that some in Israel were violating the will of God. This helps explain his "righteous anger." Not only were some of the elite in Israel ignoring the spirit of the Mosaic law, but they were also breaking the literal letter of the law. Many years earlier, God had spoken to Israel from Mount Sinai and said, "If you lend money to My people, to the poor among you, you are not to act as a creditor to him; you shall not charge him interest" (Exod. 22:25).

Furthermore, no Jew was ever to enslave another Jew. This was clear from another Old Testament passage.

> "Now in case a countryman of yours becomes poor and his means with regard to you falter [which describes specifically what had happened to some of the Jews in Nehemiah's days], then you are to sustain him, like a stranger or a sojourner, that he may live with you. *Do not take usurious interest from him,* but revere your God, that your countryman may live with you. . . . And if a countryman of yours becomes so poor with regard to you that he sells himself to you, *you shall not subject him to a slave's service.* He shall be with you as a hired man, as if he were a sojourner; . . . until the year of jubilee. He shall then go out from you, he and his sons with him, and shall go back to his family, that he may return to the property of his forefathers." (Lev. 25:35–36, 39–41)

Nehemiah vented his anger then not just at people in Israel who were exploiting others but at a violation of God's instructions. While they were praying to God for help and assistance in rebuilding the wall (which God was granting freely, and without interest), they were ignoring His commands. Their exploitation not only involved their fellow Jews, but their God.

This Called for Serious Action!

Nehemiah wasted no time in confronting the situation (5:7–11). As a spiritual leader in Israel, he had no choice if he wanted to be in the will of God himself. God had called him not only to rebuild the walls of Jerusalem, but to make sure the people obeyed His laws.

He "Held a Great Assembly Against Them"

What was happening in Israel was widespread knowledge. Consequently, Nehemiah had to deal with it publicly. This is why he "held a great assembly against them" (v. 7). He "set up a pulpit" and rebuked those who were violating God's commands. He "contended with the nobles and the rulers and said to them, 'You are exacting usury, each from his brother!'" (v. 7).

He Pulled No Punches

Nehemiah dealt with Israel's inconsistencies and hypocrisy. He reminded them of what he and others had done to help their brothers who had gone into exile. "We according to our ability," he shouted, "have redeemed our Jewish brothers who were sold to the nations; now would you even sell your brothers that they may be sold to us?" (v. 8).

In essence, Nehemiah made it clear that he and others had been paying money out of their own pockets to free these people from their pagan masters. And now their own brothers had come along and sold them again so they would have to be redeemed a second time—and this time from Jews themselves!

Right Is Right and Wrong Is Wrong

"The thing which you are doing is not good; should you not walk in the fear of our God because of the reproach of the nations, our enemies?" Nehemiah asked (v. 9).

With this question, Nehemiah showed that God's name and reputation were at stake. He had no choice but to deal with their sin. They must change their immoral and unethical behavior so they would not bring reproach on the One who delivered them from both Egyptian bondage and Babylonian captivity. Nehemiah's message was clear! Right is right and wrong is wrong!

"Won't You Do the Same?"

Nehemiah's final point was intensely personal. He referred to his own example and that of others who were helping those in need. "Look," he said, "my brothers and I and our servants are actually lending them money and grain—and without interest. Won't you do the same?" (v. 10, author's paraphrase).

True to his convictions, Nehemiah did not ask the children of Israel to do something he was not doing himself. This is why Nehemiah was such an outstanding spiritual leader. He was a man of character! He modeled integrity and loathed hypocrisy!

"Return What You Have Taken"

As Nehemiah concluded his message, he didn't allow those who were guilty of exploitation to get off the hook. He demanded they return what they had taken—"their fields, their vineyards, their olive groves, and their houses." They were also to return the interest they were "exacting from them" (v. 11).

Many years later, Jesus told His disciples that if they indeed loved Him they would obey Him (see John 15:10). He also told them to love their neighbors as themselves (see Matt. 22:39). Here in this Old Testament setting, Nehemiah told God's people the very same thing. If they really loved God and appreciated what He had done for them, they would obey His laws and have compassion on those who were not as fortunate as they.

"Don't Wait Another Day"

Nehemiah concluded his message with a sense of urgency. He didn't ask them to go home and think about what they had done and to consider how they might rectify the situation. He didn't even ask them to spend time in prayer. Rather, he said, "Please give back to them *this very day* their fields, their vineyards, their olive groves, and their houses, also the hundredth part of the money and of the grain, the new wine, and the oil that you are exacting from them" (v. 11). In other words, Nehemiah exhorted his people to deal with their sins immediately! They weren't even to wait another day!

"We Will Do Exactly as You Say"

Imagine the joy and relief that must have surged through Nehemiah's emotional veins when the people responded positively to his exhortations (vv. 12–13). What remained of his initial anger must have dissipated. "We will give it back and will require nothing from them," they responded; "we will do exactly as you say" (v. 12).

"Prove It!"

Nehemiah took one final step. He asked them to promise publicly in the presence of the spiritual leaders in Israel that they would actually do what they said they would do (see v. 12).

Nehemiah knew that words are cheap and easy to utter on the spur of the moment; particularly under public pressure. This is why he asked them to take a public oath.

To seal this oath, he graphically visualized for them the grave consequences that could come if they lied to God. He used his own garment as a visual demonstration—shaking it out. At this point, he must have once again raised his voice and shouted, "Thus may God shake out every man from his house and from his possessions who does not fulfill this promise; even thus may he be shaken out and emptied" (v. 13).

Becoming God's Man Today

Principles to Live By

We've already alluded to several powerful lessons that we can learn from Nehemiah's approach in dealing with this conflict in Israel. But let's be more specific.

Principle 1. Internal problems are inevitable.

Wherever you have a situation where people are in close association—even Christian people—you will experience internal problems. There is no perfect family, no perfect church, no perfect organization.

This is particularly true in the church. Satan will see to it. It's strange, but some people don't really seem to believe this is true. I've met people who actually seem to be looking for the perfect church—not realizing, of course, that when they arrive on the scene, the church will cease to be perfect.

On the other hand, it's God's will that internal problems be minimal. When they arise, He wants us to solve them. We have the resources at our disposal to defeat Satan's attempts to destroy our human relationships.

This principle applies as well to Israel—even in Nehemiah's day. Had they obeyed God's laws in the first place, they would not have created the internal turmoil that existed. Conversely, when they responded to Nehemiah's message and obeyed God's law, the problem was resolved.

Principle 2. We must not ignore internal conflicts.

One of the most beautiful illustrations of conflict resolution in the New Testament happened in the church in Jerusalem. The church was growing by leaps and bounds. Thousands were being converted to Jesus Christ among both those who lived in the Jerusalem area and those who had come for the fifty-day celebration prior to the Day of Pentecost. In the process, the communal system the Christians set up to meet each other's needs was being put to the test. Though it appears they had enough food, they hadn't organized well enough to keep up with the needs—particularly of the Grecian widows who had come from outside Jerusalem.

The apostles immediately recognized the problem. The Grecian Jews were complaining that their widows were being neglected in the daily distribution. Consequently, "the twelve" instructed the Grecians to select "seven men of good reputation, full of the Spirit and of wisdom"—men they could appoint to take care of this need (Acts 6:2–3).

The solution worked! Seven men were appointed and faithfully resolved the conflict. As a result, "the word of God kept on spreading; and the number of disciples continued to increase greatly in Jerusalem, and a great many of the priests were becoming obedient to the faith" (v. 7).

Imagine what would have happened if the apostles had not dealt with this conflict. We would have had the first major church split. Unresolved conflict always makes the problem worse. This is both illustrated in Scripture and in everyday life.

Guidelines to Preserving Peace

As Christians we have at our disposal all the divine resources we need to face internal problems and resolve them. We simply need to obey what God says. Following are some very important biblical guidelines that will help us to "preserve the unity of the Spirit in the bond of peace:"

➤ "[Lay] aside falsehood, speak truth, each one of you, with his neighbor, for we are members of one another" (Eph. 4:25).

➤ "Be angry, and yet do not sin; do not let the sun go down on your anger, and do not give the devil an opportunity" (vv. 26–27).

➤ "Let him who steals steal no longer; but rather let him labor, performing with his own hands what is good, in order that he may have something to share with him who has need" (v. 28).

➤ "Let no unwholesome word proceed from your mouth, but only such a word as is good for edification according to the need of the moment, that it may give grace to those who hear" (v. 29).

➤ "Let all bitterness and wrath and anger and clamor and slander be put away from you, along with all malice" (v. 31).

➤ "Be kind to one another, tender-hearted, forgiving each other" (v. 32).

Dealing with Personal Offense

Jesus Christ gives us another guideline for dealing with personal problems that often create internal strife. He said:

"And if your brother sins [against you], go and reprove him in private; if he listens to you, you have won your brother. But if he does not listen to you, take one or two more with you, so that by the mouth of two or three witnesses every fact may be confirmed. And if he refuses to listen to them, tell it to the church [a larger assembly]; and if he refuses to listen even to the church, let him be to you as a Gentile and a tax-gatherer." (Matt. 18:15–17)

This guideline alone is an important key to conflict resolution. If we would faithfully follow it, there would be few internal problems that could not be solved quickly, both within the family and within the church.

Principle 3. We must handle negative emotions properly that are caused by internal conflict.

Internal strife always causes negative emotions, both in the leader and in others. For example, Nehemiah's anger was directly related to the deep distress that he saw among the people who were being exploited and hurt.

As leaders, we must be prepared to handle these negative emotions constructively and biblically. Here Nehemiah gives us an excellent model. He didn't act on his anger until he got perspective. Though the problems we face may not be as complex, nor our emotions as intense, he gives us a wonderful example for handling our own personal anger.

First, we must understand the nature of our anger. Is it based on facts? Do I understand the circumstances leading to the conflict? Am I personally reacting because I'm hurt or threatened—or are there justifiable reasons for my anger?

Second, we all need time to reflect and gain perspective. This is imperative before we take action. Like Nehemiah, we need to get some distance on the problem. Time has a way of clearing away emotional fog and helping us to think more objectively.

Most of us will never face the kind of conflict Nehemiah faced. He was dealing with social injustice. The elite in Israel were engaging in flagrant sin by violating very clear, direct statements and commands from God. Consequently, even though his anger was justified, he still did not act on impulse—which usually creates more problems than solutions.

The Day I Lost Control

I remember attending a football game in Texas Stadium several years ago. As sometimes happens, a man was sitting in front of us who was imbibing too much alcohol. As the game progressed, so did the nature of his language. To make matters worse, every time the Cowboys advanced the ball, he stood up in front of us and blocked our view. In the process, he shouted obscenities at another fan who was sitting directly behind me.

Admittedly, my anger level was rising by degrees. I was upset because my family members were being subjected to his disgraceful behavior. Of course, the fact that he was blocking my vision didn't help either.

Unfortunately, I tried to take matters into my own hands without "consulting myself" or anybody else—including the Lord. Predictably, my communication wasn't well received—which caused him to stand up, face me and become physical. Instinctively, I stood up to protect myself—and to a casual observer it looked as if I may even have initiated the encounter.

When the stadium guard came on the scene, he didn't have a clue as to what was happening. Consequently, he told us both in no uncertain terms that if we didn't straighten up, he'd throw both of us out on our ear!

Fortunately, people around me came to my rescue and explained the situation to the guard. But as I have reflected on that experience, I see now how I could have handled the situation much differently and with much less embarrassing results for me and my whole family. Had I "consulted with myself"—as Nehemiah did—I would have simply reported the situation to the proper authorities. They would have handled the problem—and much less emotionally than I had.

Remember then that internal problems always cause negative emotions—particularly anger—but we should handle this anger in a biblical way or we will intensify and accentuate the problem. This is particularly true in a group of people meeting together for public discussion and action. There's no quicker way to lose respect than to lose control in a larger social setting.

Powerful Proverbs!

Following are some excellent Proverbs for dealing with anger in ourselves and others:

> ➤ "A man who lacks judgment derides his neighbor, but a man of understanding holds his tongue" (11:12, NIV).

> ➤ "A patient man has great understanding, but a quick-tempered man displays folly" (14:29, NIV).

> ➤ "A gentle answer turns away wrath, but a harsh word stirs up anger" (15:1).

> ➤ "A hot-tempered man stirs up dissension, but a patient man calms a quarrel" (15:18, NIV).

Principle 4. In solving conflicts among people, we must lead by example.

This is another great lesson we can learn from Nehemiah. One of the primary reasons he was successful in handling a very intense and difficult situation is that he exemplified with his own life what he asked others to do. He used his own personal actions toward the poor to illustrate obedience to God's laws.

A Lifestyle

This was a trait that characterized Nehemiah's life. When he asked them to rebuild the walls, he worked alongside them. When he asked them to pray, he prayed. When he asked them to trust God, he trusted God. When he asked them to work night and day, so did he. And—in this instance—when he asked them to help the poor, he had already helped the poor.

This principle applies to most of our relationships as Christians, particularly when we're in a leadership role. For example, as parents, we must consistently visualize and dramatize for our children our expectations. "Do as I say and not as I do" is a destructive philosophy of leadership in every arena—in the home, in the church, and in our vocational settings.

A Personal Goal

I have set this as a goal for my own life. Though I don't always live up to my own standards as I should, I try—as a spiritual leader—never to ask people to do something I am not willing to do myself. If I expect people to live a consistent Christian life, I know that I must live a consistent Christian life. If I encourage people to share their faith with non-Christians, I know that I must share my faith as well. If I exhort people to pray, I, too, must pray. If I ask people to be good stewards of God's gifts and talents, I must be a good steward of God's gifts and talents. If I ask people to give sacrificially to a special project, I must also give sacrificially to that project.

Being an example is indeed basic to being an effective pastor, parent, or person. Nehemiah illustrates it beautifully and graphically in his leadership of Israel. The apostle Paul exemplified it in his own life when he wrote to the Corinthians: "Be imitators of me, just as I also am of Christ" (1 Cor. 11:1). And on another occasion, he wrote to the Thessalonians with a similar message—"You are witnesses, and so is God, how devoutly and uprightly and blamelessly we behaved toward you believers" (1 Thess. 2:10). What a practical goal this is for every Christian living today!

Becoming a Man Who Leads by Example

As you evaluate the following principles, pray and ask the Holy Spirit to impress on your heart one lesson you need to apply more effectively in your life. Then write out a specific goal. For example, you may recognize that you don't handle anger properly.

➤ Internal problems are inevitable.

➤ We must not ignore internal conflict.

➤ We must handle negative emotions properly that are caused by internal conflict.

➤ In solving conflicts among people, we must lead by example.

Set a Goal

With God's help, I will begin immediately to carry out the following goal in my life:

_____

_____

_____

_____

Memorize the Following Scripture

Do nothing from selfishness or empty conceit, but with humility of mind let each of you regard one another as more important than himself; do not merely look out for your own personal interests, but also for the interests of others.

PHILIPPIANS 2:3–4

Chapter 9
_____

Promotion with a Proper Perspective
Read Nehemiah 5:14–19

*T*he foreman was a hardworking, conscientious man, but he had not received a promotion for ten years. Asked if he had an explanation for his failure to advance, he replied, "Many years ago I had an argument with my superior. I won."

We live in a society that thrives on promotion. We expect it! We work hard for it. It means power and prestige—and more money. Advancement is a part of our culture, particularly in the workforce.

Unfortunately, the man who was bypassed for ten years didn't "play by the rules." Advancement usually only happens when we're in good favor with those above us. And if we manage to "climb the ladder," we're in the driver's seat—at least in relationship to those below us!

This represents the average man's perspective on promotion in our society. Sound familiar? Unfortunately, it's sometimes difficult to live out our Christian convictions and "play by the world's rules." They're often in conflict.

From Foreman to Governor

I believe Nehemiah can help us all. He demonstrates strength of character in times of advancement as well as in days of adversity. His perspective on promotion provides us with another wonderful model.

Nehemiah was apparently appointed governor of Jerusalem as they were entering the homestretch in completing the wall. At that moment in Israel's history, there was no higher position of leadership.

His memoirs—which he wrote later—give us powerful insights as to how he viewed this important responsibility.

Nehemiah's rationale for inserting this descriptive paragraph (5:14–19) at this point in his journal was apparently prompted by the events he described in the previous paragraph (vv. 1–13). When he was appointed governor, he discovered that the elite of Israel were selfishly exploiting the poor. As we've seen in our previous chapter, he dealt with this problem immediately and resolved it.

As Nehemiah described the social injustice in Israel and how he handled it, he decided to "jump ahead" in his historical account and talk briefly about his experience as governor of Jerusalem. What he describes is definitely sequential—but keep in mind it represents a twelve-year period of time.

Promotion and Perks!

Promotion normally brings privileges. This was true in Nehemiah's case. He had a liberal food allowance. This was part of his "expense account" to do official entertaining. However, Nehemiah chose not to use this privilege—even though it was rightfully his—during the entire twelve years that he served as governor. He made this clear in his journal: "Moreover, from the day that I was appointed to be their governor in the land of Judah, from the twentieth year to the thirty-second year of King Artaxerxes, *for twelve years,* neither I nor my kinsmen have eaten the governor's food allowance" (v. 14).

This didn't mean that Nehemiah had no need to entertain. He still fed 150 Jews regularly at his own table—men and officials who were part of his staff. He also regularly entertained visiting dignitaries from the surrounding nations (see v. 17).

Imagine the amount of food and drink this took every day! In fact, you don't have to use your imagination. Nehemiah spelled it out: "Now that which was prepared for each day was one ox and six choice sheep, also birds were prepared for me; and once in ten days all sorts of wine were furnished in abundance. Yet for all this I did not demand the governor's food allowance, because the servitude was heavy on this people" (v. 18).

Didn't Nehemiah deserve to use his "expense account"? Wouldn't it have been legitimate? The answer is a decided "yes!" But—as Nehemiah already noted—he had his reasons, which we'll look at in more depth in a moment. But first, take a look at two very important observations regarding Nehemiah's personal example as governor of Jerusalem.

Avoiding Guilt by Association

It's true that promotion brings privileges. Unfortunately, it also provides unique opportunities to take advantage of those privileges. This is exactly what previous governors had done. "But the former governors who were before me laid burdens on the people and took from them bread and wine besides forty shekels of silver; even their servants domineered the people. But I did not do so because of the fear of God" (v. 15).

Nehemiah didn't detail everything these men had done to abuse their privileges. However, we're told enough to conclude that they took advantage of their position of power and used it to pad their own pockets. They developed a profit-sharing scheme for their servants who were charged with the responsibility to collect both money and produce from the children of Israel.

This was an insidious system. The more food and money the servants could bring into the governor's coffers, the bigger their own personal cut. Understandably, this would lead to incredible exploitation!

In the New Testament, Zacchaeus exemplifies this kind of exploitation. He was a chief tax collector—which means he had a number of tax collectors who served him. Consequently, he received a percentage of everything they collected from the people. Again, the system was corrupt. The more they could collect, the more they could keep for themselves.

When a man becomes more interested in serving God than making money, you know something unusual must have happened. Zacchaeus came face to face with Jesus Christ and His way of life. He was changed from the inside out. He acknowledged his unethical and dishonest behavior; moreover, he was willing to make right what he had done wrong. "Behold, Lord, half of my possessions I will give to the poor, and if I have defrauded anyone of anything, I will give back four times as much" (Luke 19:8).

Nehemiah, of course, cannot be compared with Zacchaeus. But those who led Israel before him can. They often exploited people through a very similar system. This is why Nehemiah reported that those before him "laid burdens on the people" and "even their servants domineered the people" (v. 15). In actuality, they were thieves and crooks!

A Conflict of Interest

Those who abuse privileges often are guilty of a conflict of interest. It would have been very easy for Nehemiah to fall into this trap. Once appointed governor, he could have concentrated on lending people money to pay their taxes, using their land as collateral. And then—when they couldn't pay back what they had borrowed—he could have applied the standard of the world and taken back their land. Like his predecessors, he could have found it easy to exploit the poor. He could have literally made them his personal slaves.

As we've seen, Nehemiah chose "the higher road"! He refused to take advantage of the people. This was what Nehemiah meant when he wrote, "We did not buy any land." Rather, he described his approach as follows: "I also applied myself to the work on this wall . . . and *all my servants* were gathered there for the work" (v. 16). In other words, Nehemiah did not use those who served him to take advantage of others. He had them working beside him rather than out exploiting the people.

If Nehemiah had followed the example of those who led the people before him, he would have been in direct violation of the Word of God. Nehemiah was in Jerusalem to uphold the law, not to violate it. He was there to help the people, not to exploit them. He was there to rebuild the wall, not to build a personal empire. Consequently, he did everything he could to avoid even an appearance that might be interpreted as a conflict of interest.

A High Calling

What motivated Nehemiah not only to *avoid abusing* his privileges as governor but also to *avoid using* the privileges that were legitimately his? His choices relate directly to how he viewed his leadership role. He considered his task a high calling from God Himself! Consequently, he conducted himself so as to reflect the character of the One he served!

He Feared God

In describing the way former governors had taken advantage of the people, Nehemiah expressly states that he "did not do so *because of the fear of God*" (v. 15b). He knew it was wrong—that it violated the law of God. More so, it would violate the very nature of God.

Nehemiah was committed to obeying God and doing His will in every respect. He could not and would not abuse his privileges as governor. This is why he also became so furious at the nobles and rulers in Israel who were exploiting the poor by lending them money, charging them exorbitant interest rates, and then confiscating their land and enslaving them when they had nothing left to pay off their debts.

Nehemiah knew that God ultimately would not tolerate this kind of behavior among the leaders in Israel. He wanted God's blessing on his life—not a curse!

He Was Sensitive to People's Needs

Again, Nehemiah made his motive clear in his historical record. When he described the amount of food he served regularly, he quickly added, "Yet for all this I did not demand the governor's food allowance, *because the servitude was heavy on this people*" (v. 18).

For years, the children of Israel had been struggling against their enemies. Their morale was at an all-time low. They barely had enough food to feed themselves, and at times they went hungry. Added to these difficulties was the challenge of trying to accomplish the impossible—to rebuild the wall of Jerusalem. Under these circumstances—even though he was entitled to special privileges as governor—Nehemiah's conscience would not allow him to lay this extra burden on the people. If they were willing to sacrifice their own personal resources and their own personal comforts to achieve God's will, He chose to remove this additional burden. Rather, Nehemiah apparently picked up the tab out of his own personal resources.

He Wanted God's Special Blessing

Nehemiah didn't hesitate to let us know that part of his motivation for doing what was right as a leader in Israel is that he wanted God's special blessing. Thus he wrote—"Remember me, O my God, for good according to all that I have done for this people" (5:19; cf. 13:14, 22, 31).

The Babylonian captivity was still very fresh in Nehemiah's mind. We learned from his prayer recorded in chapter 1 that he remembered clearly that God had promised Israel "blessings" if they obeyed Him but a "curse" if they did not (Neh. 1:8–9; Deut. 28:1–68). Nehemiah clearly desired a blessing rather than a curse!

No doubt Nehemiah's memory went back even further—to what God had said to Joshua as he was about ready to lead the children of Israel into the promised land:

> "Be careful to do according to all the law which Moses My servant commanded you; do not turn from it to the right or to the left, so *that you may have success wherever you go.* This book of the law shall not depart from your mouth [that is, you should teach it consistently], but you shall meditate on it day and night, so that you may be careful to do according to all that is written in it; *for then you will make your way prosperous, and then you will have success."* (Josh. 1:7–8)

Becoming God's Man Today

Principles to Live By

Nehemiah's experience and example as governor of Jerusalem speaks clearly to every one of us who lives and works in our own communities. If we do our jobs well, we'll normally experience advancement—which brings increased responsibilities. It's part of our social and economic system—and we certainly wouldn't want it any other way. But how can we accept promotion with a proper Christian perspective?

Principle 1. We should consider accepting a promotion as a potential blessing from God.

Some Christians are afraid of advancement—particularly positions that involve authority and increased responsibility. We may fear failure—which is natural for most of us. Or, we may not want to accept the accountability that goes with responsibility. And then, some Christians feel that advancement is somehow wrong and inappropriate—that, in some respects, we're to be "seen and not heard." These are not valid reasons for rejecting a promotion.

Obviously, we must think carefully before we accept increased responsibility. For example, on the long haul, increased income and benefits may not compensate for the demands that are placed upon us and the price we have to pay in terms of time and effort. It's not wrong to count the cost, particularly when it affects our biblical priorities. For example, it's never right to sacrifice our family on the altar of promotion. That's too great a price to pay!

On the other hand, whether or not we accept a promotion should be based upon more than the way it will affect us personally. It must also be based upon more than an increased salary and other benefits. *We must evaluate the opportunity in terms of what God can do through us!*

Principle 2. We should consider accepting a promotion because it may give us an opportunity for personal growth.

Increased leadership responsibility stretches us in a number of ways. It provides us with opportunities to increase our faith. Like Nehemiah, we will learn to pray more effectively. We will also develop our potential as we learn new skills. Promotions always give us opportunities to develop our abilities to relate to other people and to raise our tolerance level for handling difficult situations.

True, increased responsibility always brings periods of emotional pain, but without these experiences we tend to maintain the status quo. We actually need a certain amount of stress to cause us to grow spiritually and psychologically. This was why James wrote: "Consider it all joy, my brethren, when you encounter various trials knowing that the testing of your faith produces endurance. And let endurance have its perfect result, that you may be perfect and complete, lacking in nothing" (James 1:2–4).

Principle 3. We should consider accepting a promotion because it may improve our financial situation.

It is not wrong to make money. When we have enough to live comfortably, it frees us from worry and concern and increases our security in life. In turn, this will enable us to be more productive. Rather than dissipating our energies through worry, we can focus our energies on honoring and glorifying God.

More importantly, an increased income enables us to give more to meet others' needs and to advance the work of God. For those who have learned the joy of giving, it not only provides personal blessings, but untold blessings for those who are recipients of their graciousness. God makes it very clear that we are to give proportionately as we prosper (see 1 Cor. 16:2).

So don't feel guilty about making money. Accept it as a blessing from God. However, be on guard. It's easy to "love money"—and when we do, we are no longer seeking "first His kingdom and His righteousness" (Matt. 6:33). Our priorities are out of order.

Principle 4. We should consider accepting a promotion since it may provide us with an opportunity to create working conditions that will benefit and help others.

We definitely need more Christians directing the affairs of life. Proverbs tells us, "When the righteous increase, the people rejoice, but when a wicked man rules, people groan" (Prov. 29:2).

May God give us more godly people who have significant responsibilities at all levels in our society—in the business world, in educational institutions, in the political arena, and, perhaps most important of all, in the church.

Principle 5. When we accept a promotion, we must realize that we will face new temptations.

This does not mean we should not accept a promotion. Rather, we must simply be on guard. This is especially true if the position brings with it unusual privileges—such as it did when Nehemiah became governor of Jerusalem. Because this was the highest position in Israel, it opened the door of temptation to many governors before Nehemiah, who—seemingly without giving it a second thought—walked through the door and abused their privileges.

Thomas Carlyle, a Scottish historian, once wrote, "Adversity is hard on a man; but for one man who can stand prosperity, there are a hundred that will stand adversity."[1]

Charles Swindoll keyed off on the same idea:

> Few people can live in the lap of luxury and maintain their spiritual, emotional, and moral equilibrium. Sudden elevation often disturbs balance, which leads to pride and a sense of self-sufficiency—and then, a fall. It's ironic, but more of us can hang tough through a demotion than through a promotion. And it is at this level a godly leader shows himself or herself strong. The right kind of leaders, when promoted, know how to handle the honor.[2]

These statements may be scary, but that's all right! Knowing the facts about temptations simply help us to be humble and to be on guard. Nehemiah illustrates with his life that a man can serve in a high position and yet remain true to God—which leads us to additional principles that flow from his life and that will enable us to handle promotion and advancement in a godly fashion.

Principle 6. When promoted, we must never abuse our privileges.

Practically speaking, this means we must never use our position as a platform to "promote" ourselves. Most everyone who is promoted to a position in top management in our own culture faces these temptations regularly. With advancement comes trust and new freedom. If we're not committed to certain values, we can misuse expense accounts, exploit people to further our own personal interests, and use company time to build our own personal empire.

Let's remember that Nehemiah faced these temptations. The opportunity was there. Other governors before him had done it all. In fact, the people probably even expected it to happen again. But Nehemiah refused to fall prey to selfish ambition. What a great lesson for all of us who live and work in today's world!

Principle 7. When promoted, we might be wise to give up certain rights so as to avoid any "appearance of evil"—or to simply be a good example.

Nehemiah gave up his rights because of the economic conditions in Israel when he became governor. In actuality, he could have insisted on his food allowance and no one would have questioned his actions or his motives. But as we've seen, he refused to use this right because the people were facing hard economic times. He had also asked them to personally sacrifice in order to rebuild the walls. And since he had sufficient personal resources to care for the food allowance himself, he did not insist on using this privilege.

Should We Ever Give Up Rights Today?

I personally believe there are opportunities in our society today—especially in the Christian community—when we can give up rights to avoid being misinterpreted. Paul illustrates this dramatically in his own ministry. He often gave up his own privileges as an apostle so as to help people understand more clearly that the gospel is a free gift of God. He made this clear when he wrote to the Corinthians:

> Am I not free? Am I not an apostle? . . . Do we not have a
> right to eat and drink? . . . Who at any time serves as a soldier at
> his own expense? Who plants a vineyard, and does not eat the fruit
> of it? Or who tends a flock and does not use the milk of the flock?
> . . . If we sowed spiritual things in you, is it too much if we should
> reap material things from you? If others share the right over you,

do we not more? Nevertheless, we did not use this right, but we endure all things, that we may cause no hindrance to the gospel of Christ. (1 Cor. 9:1, 4, 7, 11–12)

In this sense, Nehemiah was an Old Testament "apostle Paul." He gave up his own rights in order to achieve God's purposes on earth. Though this is certainly not a normal expectation from people in leadership, I believe there are times when it is the best thing to do. It's a true test of our motives.

A Personal Experience

I seldom share this experience lest I be misinterpreted and lest people expect all Christian leaders to do the same. However, in this context, I believe it's appropriate.

I made a decision a number of years ago to set up a special benevolence account that could be monitored by my fellow elders in the church I serve. This account is funded by the monies I receive from speaking engagements other than my regular salary as a full-time pastor.

I had several purposes in doing this. *First,* I receive a lot of invitations to speak in various places. Frankly, I didn't want to make the decision to accept or reject these invitations based on the amount of money I could receive. I'm sure it's not surprising that the decision to set up a special account has indeed removed that temptation. I can honestly say that since setting up this fund, I have never made a decision based upon the amount of remuneration offered. What a freeing experience this is!

Second, I did not want to become guilty of a conflict of interest. Since I was being paid a fair salary to serve the people in my church on a full-time basis, I didn't want to be tempted to be spending time elsewhere generating a "second income" while neglecting to be a "laborer worthy of my hire" in my own church family. Again, since making that decision, I've eliminated this temptation as well as the guilt that should always accompany a conflict of interest. This, too, is a liberating experience.

Third, I wanted to set up a fund that I could use to minister to people who could not afford paying my travel expenses and paying honorarium for ministry. Since that time, I've often been able to use these monies to travel to various parts of the world to minister freely to missionaries and other groups. This, of course, has generated incredible joy in my heart—since in addition to tithing from my regular income, I have monies to use for additional ministry.

Please don't misunderstand! I'm not suggesting this is a policy that other Christian leaders should set up. I'm convinced that most pastors deserve additional income and certainly most are not guilty of a conflict of interest. But it is a temptation for Christian leaders who are in great demand. Like Nehemiah, I did not want to fall prey to this kind of behavior. Consequently, I gave up these rights.

Also understand that I was never asked to make this decision. I did so based on what I felt was a biblical principle lived out by men like Nehemiah and the apostle Paul, who gave up rights so as never to be accused of taking advantage of others— and of the grace of God! I have never regretted this decision!

Principle 8. We should always accept a promotion with proper motives.

We've seen that Nehemiah was motivated by three factors as he carried out his work as governor. He feared God, he was sensitive to people's needs, and he desired God's special blessing in his life. If we approach advancement and promotion with these same basic motivations, we, too, will have the key to maintaining our spiritual and psychological equilibrium.

Fearing God

Unfortunately, many Christians today ignore this important spiritual guideline. One reason is that we take God's promise of blessing upon the righteous and unrighteous for granted (see Matt. 5:45). Sometimes we also use "fear" inappropriately—giving Christians the impression that God is ready to pounce on us and punish us the moment we disobey Him. We do not balance the "fear of God" with the "love of God."

On the other hand, we often go to the other extreme and ignore God's Word. Because He doesn't reach down out of heaven and deal with us directly, we take His grace for granted.

Today, we need more godly fear. Rightly defined, this means we should stand in awe of who God is and what He's done for us—and that eventually we will have to give an account to Him for how we have lived our lives on earth.

Sensitivity to People

If as Christians we are sensitive to others, we'll not take advantage of them. We'll never use our positions of power to exploit people. Rather, we'll use these opportunities to help people—to make their lives more comfortable and to create better living and working conditions. Our goal will be that of Christ—to become a greater servant as our position of authority and power increases. When we are motivated by this kind of thinking, I'm convinced we'll be able to handle almost any promotion without succumbing to Satan's tactics.

Favored by God

It is not wrong to do good in order to be favored by God. He has promised that He will reward us. In the New Testament, the greatest emphasis is on eternal rewards, but earthly rewards are not excluded. Though they should always be secondary in terms of what motivates us as a leader, it is natural to expect blessings from God when we serve Him and others well.

Becoming a Man with Pure Motives

As you evaluate the following principles and spiritual guidelines for accepting promotion and advancement, pray and ask the

Holy Spirit to impress on your heart one lesson you need to apply more effectively in your life. Then write out a specific goal. For example, you may have concluded that you are using your position of authority inappropriately by taking advantage of others so you can enhance your own position.

➤ We should consider accepting a promotion as a potential blessing from God.

➤ We should consider accepting a promotion because it may give us an opportunity for personal growth.

➤ We should consider accepting a promotion because it may improve our financial situation.

➤ We should consider accepting a promotion since it may provide us with an opportunity to create working conditions that will benefit and help others.

➤ When we accept a promotion, we must realize that we will face new temptations.

➤ When promoted, we must never abuse our privileges.

➤ When promoted, we might be wise to give up certain rights so as to avoid any "appearance of evil"—or to simply be a good example.

➤ We should always accept a promotion with proper motives.

A Special Prayer

Dear God,
I will accept with gratitude the opportunities for advancement You allow to come my way. I will, however, count the cost to me personally, and particularly to my family so that I will not violate any biblical priorities. I will not withdraw simply because I fear failure or am unwilling to accept the accountability that accompanies the responsibility. Nor will I refuse the opportunity because of the misguided point of view that Christians should not seek or consider prestigious positions.

On the other hand, I realize that Satan will work harder in my life if I accept advancement. To counter these attacks, I will use the position as an opportunity to grow spiritually. I will consider this promotion as a better platform to also advance my Christian witness. Though I believe it is appropriate to use my improved financial situation to create a greater sense of security for my family, I will also do all I can to be a good steward and give more to advance the work of Your church. I will never abuse the privileges accompanying my promotion, financially or in any other way. I will not exploit others or become guilty of a conflict of interest.

To accomplish these goals I will discharge my responsibilities in the fear of God, realizing He alone has made this opportunity possible. I will also do all I can to use my position as a servant to others, meeting their needs and improving their lot in life. In turn, Lord, I believe You will reward me personally now and eternally because I view my work as Your work and because I have been faithful to Your principles. I will do all I can to make sure my motives honor You first and foremost and not myself.

In Jesus' name, Amen.

Signed _____

Set a Goal

With God's help, I will begin immediately to carry out the following goal in my life:

_____

_____

_____

_____

Memorize the Following Scripture

> *For you recall, brethren, our labor and hardship, how working night and day so as not to be a burden to any of you, we proclaimed to you the gospel of God. You are witnesses, and so is God, how devoutly and uprightly and blamelessly we behaved toward you believers.*
>
> 1 THESSALONIANS 2:9–10

Chapter 10

When People Try to Hurt You
Read Nehemiah 6:1–14

*M*ost of us know about Charles Colson. He went to prison because of his involvement in Watergate. But there may be an aspect of his story that you haven't heard.

When he was released, a newspaper article accused him—at least by innuendo—of being part of a murder plot against a newspaper columnist. Chuck reports that he was initially very angry. His wife, Patty, tried to cheer him up. "'What do you mean "smile"?' I growled at her. I've been accused of a lot of wild things but not murder!"

Unable to handle the problem by himself, Colson eventually sought counsel from several Christians who were his close friends and mentors. Together they considered one basic question: How does a Christian handle false accusations?

Colson's inclination was to battle back, to protest, to proclaim his innocence. The others shook their heads. "Anything you say, Chuck, will be twisted," noted one of his strongest encouragers. "Let's find out how Jesus handled these situations. He was falsely accused more times than any man in history."[1]

Later, we'll look at how Chuck Colson actually handled this painful experience. But first, let's look once again at Nehemiah who, in this next scenario, faced his most difficult test as a leader. He, too, was falsely accused. This time his enemies came as "wolves in sheep's clothing"—to paraphrase a statement from Jesus Christ (see Matt. 7:15).

The Big Picture

The children of Israel rebuilt the wall around Jerusalem in an incredible fifty-two days. Even their enemies recognized this accomplishment as a miracle engineered not only by Nehemiah and the children of Israel but by God Himself (see Neh. 6:16).

However, during this brief but action-packed period, the children of Israel faced some difficult problems. Not only did they have to sacrifice time, energy, and personal resources, but they encountered intense opposition from their enemies who repeatedly tried to stop the building process.

"They Mocked and Despised Us"

The majority of these attacks were precipitated by Sanballat the Horonite, Tobiah the Ammonite, and Geshem the Arab. When these men first heard that Nehemiah had come from Susa to Jerusalem to "seek the welfare of the sons of Israel," they were very unhappy and displeased (2:10). And when they saw the children of Israel actually "put their hands to the good work" (v. 18), they translated their displeasure into action. They "mocked and despised" God's people (v. 19).

The children of Israel were not to be denied. The more they were threatened and verbally attacked, the harder they worked. Sanballat particularly was highly threatened by all of this activity. The negative emotions he was already feeling intensified and he "became furious and very angry" (4:1)! But when his psychological strategy collapsed, he knew he had to take more direct action.

They "Conspired Together"

Sanballat huddled with Tobiah and Geshem (see v. 8). Out of this meeting came a plan to attack secretly Jerusalem from all sides (see fig. 6-1). But Nehemiah discovered their plan and he led Israel to prepare for the attack. It never happened and the work went on until the wall was completed. There was only one thing left to do—to "set up the doors in the gates" (6:1).

One Final Effort

Sanballat, Tobiah, and Geshem made one final effort to keep Nehemiah from taking this final step. It was their most subtle and insidious attack, and Nehemiah was their sole object. If they could only remove him from the scene—or at least destroy his credibility in Israel—they might have a chance once again to demoralize the people. In chapter 6, Nehemiah describes three subtle attacks on him personally. Each was different, but each was designed to destroy him—if not his life, at least his effectiveness as a leader in Israel.

A Peace Conference

The first scheme was the most subtle (6:1–4). Sanballat and Geshem invited Nehemiah to meet with them "at Chephirim in the plain of Ono" (v. 2).[2] They made it appear that they wanted to have a peace conference with Nehemiah, but their hidden motive was to harm Nehemiah—perhaps even to kill him (see v. 2).

If you were watching from the sidelines, you might conclude that they were saying, "Okay, Nehemiah! You win! Let's get together and talk. There is no need to continue a cold war. In fact, you pick the place in Ono, and we'll meet you there."

Between a Rock and a Hard Place

Nehemiah was too wise to buy into their plan. He suspected foul play—and he was right! But, he faced a dilemma. He couldn't prove that they didn't have good intentions. If he questioned their motives outright, he would only intensify their anger and, at the same time, make himself look bad in the eyes of those in Israel who were sympathetic to Tobiah (see vv. 17–19). As we'll see in our final chapter, Nehemiah had some very close relations among the children of Israel through inter-marriage—including some people in high positions. This put Nehemiah between a "rock and a hard place."

Though Nehemiah couldn't prove that his enemies' motives were anything but pure, he responded as we would expect this man of God to respond. He didn't allow this predicament to cloud his thinking, which enabled him to choose a method that would eventually demonstrate whether or not they *were sincere.* He simply "sent messengers to them, saying, 'I am doing a great work and I cannot come down. Why should the work stop while I leave it and come down to you?'" (v. 3).

Nehemiah's response and questions were logical and reason-able. He kept his cool! He wasn't openly questioning their motives. Anyone who knew what was happening in Jerusalem would accept his response at face value. In fact, "thinking" people would conclude that he gave these men an opportunity to demonstrate that their motives *were sincere*—that they really wanted to make peace. After all, it would be just as easy—if not easier—for them to come to him.

They "Tipped Their Hand"

Nehemiah's enemies were not about to meet him in Jerusa-lem. In fact, they stepped up their pressure on Nehemiah to meet them in the plain of Ono. They sent the same message four times—and four times Nehemiah responded by telling them that he couldn't leave his work. In reality, he was giving them an opportunity to prove that their motives were pure.

Think for a moment how easy it would have been for Nehemiah—upon the third or fourth request—to attack their motives, to accuse them of insincerity in an attempt to harm him. But he didn't. He patiently waited it out, hoping they would clearly reveal what was in their hearts—and that's exactly what happened.

A Pressure Tactic

Sanballat and Geshem soon got the "real message" (vv. 5–9). Nehemiah wasn't about to leave Jerusalem and meet with them at a so-called "peace conference." Consequently, they tried another tactic. They put pressure on him, trying to force him to meet with them in the plain of Ono. Sanballat sent his servant to read an open letter to Nehemiah:

> "It is reported among the nations, and Gashmu [Geshem] says, that you and the Jews are planning to rebel; therefore you are rebuilding the wall. And you are to be their king, according to these reports. And you have also appointed prophets to proclaim in Jerusalem concerning you, 'A king is in Judah!' And now it will be reported to the king according to these reports. So come now, let us take counsel together." (vv. 6–7)

Analyze this letter carefully and you'll see several subtle and insidious elements.

Sanballat's Corrupt Tactics

1. They wanted it to appear that they had Nehemiah's welfare at heart. How clever! Sanballat and Geshem designed this letter to convey the idea that they knew these reports were just rumors—but they made it very clear that if King Artaxerxes heard about what was happening in Jerusalem, he definitely wouldn't know they were rumors. And if that happened, he'd be very unhappy! In other words, they wanted Nehemiah to get the impression that their desire to get together was to discuss the matter in order to protect Nehemiah. Obviously, this was not their intent.

2. They were attempting to get Nehemiah to respond out of fear. Sanballat and Geshem knew only too well that King Artaxerxes trusted Nehemiah to be a loyal subject. Otherwise he would not have authorized him to come to Jerusalem. Under these circumstances, Nehemiah's normal reaction would be to protect himself against this possible misunderstanding. His enemies were hoping this would bring him to the bargaining table.

3. They probably included an element of truth in this letter. This is their most subtle tactic. It's quite possible that some well-meaning religious leaders in Judah had interpreted Nehemiah's presence and accomplishments in Jerusalem as a fulfillment of some of the Old Testament prophecies regarding the coming king and messiah. For example, some patriotic preacher may have spoken on Zechariah 9:9—"Behold, your king is coming to you; He is just and endowed with salvation." It's easy to see how someone may have applied this statement about Jesus Christ to Nehemiah. After all, at that moment, he appeared to be their deliverer.

4. They put pressure on Nehemiah to respond by having his letter read publicly. We don't know who heard this letter read, but we do know that it was an "open letter." The people who were listening casually could easily interpret what was said as suggesting a good course of action to protect not only Nehemiah but all of Israel. After all, if these reports *did* get back to King Artaxerxes, he could very quickly issue a decree—as he had done before—to stop the work. This time he might take more serious action against the Jews. There's no doubt what it would mean for Nehemiah. He could be sentenced to death.

Nehemiah's Response

Nehemiah quickly saw through their second scheme. It was just another trick. However, this time his enemies opened the door for him to be much more direct and straightforward with his response. The "weight of evidence" as to what was really true was shifting in his direction.

1. He denied the accusations. Nothing could be further from the truth. Nehemiah and the Jews were *not* "planning to rebel." This was not why they were "rebuilding the wall." He was *not* planning to "be their king." He had *not* appointed prophets to proclaim a king is in Judah (vv. 6–7). These accusations were so bogus that it was ridiculous—and Nehemiah let them know it in no uncertain terms: "Such things as you are saying have not been done, but you are inventing them in your own mind" (6:8). With this response, Nehemiah was not being defensive. Rather, he was honestly and openly defending the truth.

2. He made his response public. These were serious charges and Nehemiah knew that the way to counter lies is to let other people know the truth and what his enemies were trying to accomplish. Consequently, he released the following statement: "For all of them were trying to frighten us, thinking, 'They will become discouraged with the work and it will not be done'" (v. 9).

3. He prayed. This is indeed "vintage Nehemiah"! He did what he had done so often before in crisis situations. He lifted his heart to God and prayed: "But now, O God, strengthen my hands" (v. 9).

Obviously, this was a difficult time for Nehemiah. He needed divine strength and help. No one takes pleasure in being openly accused falsely. No person enjoys having his motives misinterpreted. No individual feels comfortable when his "good be evil spoken of" (Rom. 14:16, KJV). And I've never met an individual who likes to be accused of being on an ego trip when the facts are that he has sacrificed greatly to help others achieve their own goals.

Hiring a Traitor

When the letter failed to get the response that Sanballat and Geshem hoped, they devised another scheme (vv. 10–14). The next plot was to try to destroy Nehemiah's credibility in Israel.

Have you noticed that Tobiah's "influence" has suddenly disappeared from the previous attempts to discredit Nehemiah? There's a reason. He had close friends and relatives on the "inside." And though his name was not mentioned in conjunction with the open letter, he'd been doing his share of communicating behind the scenes (see vv. 17–19). He simply went undercover to engineer this next evil plot. How else could they have hired a man on "the inside" to propose a solution to Nehemiah (see v. 12)?

The man they hired was Shemaiah, and he claimed to be a prophet. Part of his strategy was to purposely lock himself in his house and then to send word for Nehemiah to come visit him. He structured an urgent situation that hopefully would arouse Nehemiah's curiosity.

In some respects, this must have been more painful for Nehemiah than the other schemes. This was the ultimate in betrayal. Nehemiah must have trusted Shemaiah, for he would not have gone to visit someone secretively whom he didn't trust.

When Nehemiah arrived, Shemaiah's message was direct and to the point: "Let us meet together in the house of God, within the temple, and let us close the doors of the temple, for they are coming to kill you, and they are coming to kill you at night" (v.10).

Two Fatal Flaws

Once again, Nehemiah saw right through this scheme. They had made two serious mistakes in their plan.

1. It didn't make sense for Nehemiah to "leave the scene" at this stage of the game. The Lord had made it possible for Nehemiah to come to Jerusalem in the first place—and had protected him from his enemies during the building process. The project was almost completed—except for installing the doors and the gates.

Why would God ask Nehemiah to flee at this moment? If Nehemiah had, it would have totally destroyed the confidence Israel had in him as a leader. They wouldn't understand such actions from the one who had been their encourager. Thus Nehemiah exclaimed to Shemaiah, "Should a man like me flee?" Putting it even more dramatically, "Should the one who has been appointed by God to lead Israel to rebuild this wall suddenly turn and run?"

2. Shemaiah's "prophetic message" asked Nehemiah to violate God's law. You see, Nehemiah was not a priest. He was a layman. For him to enter and shut himself in the temple—literally within the holy place—would be to desecrate the house of God and to bring himself under God's judgment (see Num. 18:7).

It didn't take but a moment for Nehemiah to put these two fatal flaws together. He knew immediately that Shemaiah was a false prophet, employed by his enemies to trick him (see Neh. 6:12). Nehemiah later recorded in his journal that he saw clearly why all of this happened: "He was hired for this reason, that I might become frightened and act accordingly and sin, so that they might have an evil report in order that they could reproach me" (v. 13).

It's clear that Nehemiah's enemies were willing to stoop to any means to achieve their corrupt and selfish goals. Perhaps the most subtle aspect of the final scheme was to capitalize on the fears they had already generated in Nehemiah's heart. They tried to convince him that the God who had called him to Jerusalem in the first place was now telling him through Shemaiah the prophet to run for his life. And to make matters even more difficult, Shemaiah was apparently only one of several in Israel who cooperated with Sanballat and Geshem. This is why Nehemiah recorded the prayer that he had prayed at this moment in his life. Note that he now mentioned Tobiah in this prayer, indicating his undercover involvement: "Remember, O my God, *Tobiah* and *Sanballat* according to these works of theirs, and also *Noadiah* the prophetess and the *rest of the prophets who were trying to frighten me*" (v. 14).

Becoming God's Man Today

Principles to Live By

Most of us as Christians cannot identify with Nehemiah's frustrating encounters with Sanballat, Tobiah, and Geshem. There are few of us living in our culture who face threats on our lives. In fact, very few of us have enemies who deliberately and maliciously attempt to destroy our reputation and credibility—although there are some instances when this happens.

But once again, Nehemiah's responses yield some powerful principles to live by. *How* he faced these problems exemplifies for us how we can respond to all levels of human conflict—whether it involves a deceptive and malicious attack on one end of the social continuum, or naive and sincere criticism on the opposite end.

Principle 1. When criticized, we must not counterattack by questioning the other person's motives.

Perhaps the one who is criticizing us has wrong motives—but in most instances, we can't prove it. Even Nehemiah—who had every reason to question his enemies' motives on the basis of their past behavior—did not openly question what was in their hearts. Rather, he simply refused to meet with them, stating he couldn't leave his work. It wasn't just an excuse. It involved an honest and sincere priority in his life. Everyone knew this to be true.

Obviously, this did not satisfy Sanballat and the others, but it refused them the opportunity to try to convince their friends in Israel that it was Nehemiah—not they— who had an uncooperative spirit.

Remember, too, that what appears to be an inappropriate motive may actually be sincere. Though it was highly improbable that Nehemiah's enemies had undergone a change of heart, he had to allow for that possibility.

People Do Change

I'm reminded of a husband who was very insensitive to his wife and children. For years, his wife had tolerated his selfish behavior, hoping for change. Eventually, she couldn't emotionally handle the problem any more. She left her husband and filed for a divorce.

At that point, she got her husband's attention. He began to change. He indicated he was terribly sorry for his actions. He also made it very clear that he didn't want to lose his wife or his family.

Frankly, I believe that he *had* changed. He had become a different person—psychologically and spiritually. However, his estranged wife interpreted everything he did as being based on a false motive. In her mind, he couldn't be sincere. From her perspective, he had to be engaging in manipulative behavior.

This woman's fears are understandable. But it's also true that people change. And if they haven't changed—if their motives are wrong—they'll eventually reveal what's in their hearts. That's what happened in Nehemiah's situation—which is another important principle for dealing with people who are trying to manipulate us.

Principle 2. We must be patient and wait for motives to be revealed.

Nehemiah's enemies had suggested four times a peace conference, which was designed to harm him. Four times he responded by telling them he couldn't come at that point in time. The fifth time, *they* grew impatient and "tipped their hand." They changed their strategy which gave Nehemiah an opportunity to respond to concrete facts.

As Christians, we must be patient in the area of human conflict. Malicious and false motives will eventually come to the surface. Furthermore, if people are critical because they're sincerely naive, they normally will have a change of heart if we continue to be open, sincere, and nondefensive.

Remember, too, that sincere people sometimes misinterpret our motives because we aren't being wise in our own approach to relationships. I found it to be a good rule of thumb that most Christians are not out to hurt or harm other Christians. Furthermore, their criticisms are sometimes based on misunderstandings or unwise actions and responses on our part. We must not allow ourselves to become paranoid and come to the place where we believe everyone is out to get us. If we do, we'll become immobilized as leaders.

What about the wife who could no longer trust? This is a difficult question to answer. Frankly, I wish she had given her husband another chance. Though I could be wrong, I believe that he had truly changed. If his motives *were* wrong, I'm confident they would have surfaced rather quickly. However, I also understand why his wife didn't want to take another chance. In this instance, only God can judge what was right and what was wrong.

Principle 3. *When criticized by unbelievers, we should follow the teachings of the New Testament.*

The apostle Peter dealt with this problem in his first epistle. He was writing to Christians who were scattered throughout various sections of the New Testament world and who were being persecuted by non-Christians. Peter gave them some very wise instruction:

> Keep your behavior excellent among the Gentiles, *so that in the thing in which they slander you* as evildoers, they may on account of your good deeds, as they observe them, glorify God in the day of visitation. (1 Pet. 2:12)

> For such is the will of God that by doing right you may silence the ignorance of foolish men. (v. 15)

> But sanctify Christ as Lord in your hearts, always being ready to make a defense to everyone who asks you to give an account for the hope that is in you, yet with gentleness and reverence; and keep a good conscience *so that in the thing in which you are slandered,* those who revile your good behavior in Christ may be put to shame. (3:15–16)

Principle 4. *When criticized unjustly, we must be bold and honest in our responses to rumors but never take revenge.*

Nehemiah's enemies tried to harm him by starting a rumor which they hoped would force him to meet with them. His response outlines a very biblical way for us to handle this kind of public pressure. *First,* he denied the false accusations with a straightforward but nondefensive response. *Second,* he interpreted what had happened to those closest to him so that they would know the truth. And *third,* he prayed for personal strength to endure the anxiety and stress caused by these false rumors.

It was not easy for Nehemiah to face the false accusations brought against him by his enemies. This is why he prayed, "But now, O God, strengthen my hands" (6:9). Nor is it easy for any one of us to be falsely accused—to have our motives questioned. But God *can* strengthen us in times like these and actually enrich our lives. We can learn valuable lessons in the midst of this kind of pain.

Principle 5. When falsely accused, we must not allow fear to cloud our perceptions and cause us to act impulsively and do something foolish.

Nehemiah's enemies wanted to frighten him, particularly when they told him that Artaxerxes would hear this rumor. They also tried to discourage Nehemiah—to cause him to leave the work and flee, perhaps to return to Susa to prove to the king that these rumors were false. They attempted to frighten him with a false prophecy from God regarding proposed threats on his life. But in the midst of all of these accusations and rumors, Nehemiah did not allow his fear to cause him to act irrationally. Difficult as it must have been, he indeed kept his cool!

This is a tremendous lesson for all of us. How easy it is to defend ourselves—to counterattack. If we're not careful, we can spend all of our time and energy protecting our image and being sidetracked from our primary work and responsibility.

Yes, there are things we must do—as illustrated from Nehemiah's example. But beyond that, we must follow Jesus

Christ's example, which is so clearly stated in the Epistle to the Hebrews:

> Therefore, since we have so great a cloud of witnesses sur-rounding us, let us also lay aside every encumbrance, and the sin which so easily entangles us, and let us run with endurance the race that is set before us, fixing our eyes on Jesus, the author and perfecter of faith, who for the joy set before Him endured the cross, despising the shame, and has sat down at the right hand of the throne of God. For consider Him who has endured such hostility by sinners against Himself, so that you may not grow weary and lose heart. (Heb. 12:1–3)

Principle 6. When we follow God's principles for handling false accusations, He will ultimately defend us.

I found this to be true in my own life. On one occasion, I felt I had exhausted all the possibilities in dealing with some false accusations. But the problem still didn't go away. Too many people believed the rumors.

I remember clearly when I "gave up," not in the sense of running from the problem, but I "gave up" trying to defend my-self and turned the problem over to the Lord. I reminded Him it was His reputation that was really at stake. At that moment, the "cloud that covered my soul" began to lift. I could once again "see the sunshine"—first with "small rays" that broke through the clouds. Eventually, the sun was in full view. I knew then and there that God would take care of the problem in His own time.

It should not surprise us that He did. In fact, the Lord handled it in such a way that everyone who really wanted to know the truth actually knew the truth. In fact, the way the Lord handled the problem was *far more effective* than anything I could have ever done! Though I would not want to go through that experience again, I can now look back and consider it one of the greatest spiritual growth periods in my life. God did not let me down! Furthermore, I learned some valuable lessons on how to avoid that kind of problem in the future.

What About Chuck Colson?

I began this chapter by referring to some false accusations against Chuck Colson when he came out of prison. There were strong implications that he had been part of a plan that led to murder. As you'll remember, Colson met with some of his closest Christian friends. Together they faced the question, How would Jesus handle this kind of accusation? At this point, let's allow Chuck to share his response in his own words:

> The minute Harold spoke, I knew the answer. I had been reading the Beatitudes only a week before. Jesus had told His disciples: "Blessed are you when men revile you and persecute you and utter all kinds of evil against you falsely on my account. Rejoice and be glad, for your reward is great in heaven" (Matt. 5:11–12, rsv).
>
> Did this statement apply to me? Was I being falsely accused because of my stand for Christ? Far from it. Still, as a Christian, shouldn't my response to unfair accusation be the same? I was to accept the attack without defending myself. While I wasn't quite able to "rejoice and be glad" in the situation, I did turn it over to the Lord. But it was tough to do, I discovered.

As weeks passed, the story faded out of the news. But Colson was concerned that the false accusation remained in the minds of millions of people. "It is a terrifying experience," he wrote, "to be associated with a 'murder plot,' yet I see it now that this episode was used to prepare me for even more difficult testings."[3]

Chuck Colson's response was not an easy one, nor did it suddenly remove the emotional pain or the problem. But eventually, the majority of people knew the truth because of the way he lived his Christian life and through others who defended him.

This is an illustration of what Peter said would happen. Many people glorified God because they had observed "good deeds" (1 Pet. 2:12). In "doing right," Colson put to "silence the ignorance of foolish men" (v. 15). And eventually most of those who reviled his "good behavior in Christ" were put to shame (3:16).

Will This Really Work?

What worked for Nehemiah in the Old Testament, for Paul in the New Testament, and for Chuck Colson in the twentieth-century, will also work for any one of us. I know it did for me.

Let us always remember the words of Paul: "Never take your own revenge, beloved, but leave room for the wrath of God, for it is written, "'Vengeance is Mine, I will repay,' says the Lord" (Rom. 12:19). God's will is that we "not be overcome by evil," but rather that we "overcome evil with good" v. 21).

Becoming a Man Who Handles Criticism Well

Use the following inventory to determine how you respond to criticism. After each statement, ask the Holy Spirit to impress on your heart one lesson you need to apply more effectively in your life. Then write out a specific goal. For example, you may tend to question people's motives when they criticize you.

1. I am wise in the way I respond.
   Unsatisfactory 1 2 3 4 5 Satisfactory

   I do not counterattack or question others' motives.
   Unsatisfactory 1 2 3 4 5 Satisfactory

   I am patient and wait for motives to be revealed as right or wrong through actions that cannot be misinterpreted.
   Unsatisfactory 1 2 3 4 5 Satisfactory

   If falsely accused, I continue to live a consistent Christian life, knowing that eventually I will be vindicated in the eyes of those who are seeking truth.
   Unsatisfactory 1 2 3 4 5 Satisfactory

   I learn from these experiences, realizing I may bring some of this on myself because of my own unwise behavior.
   Unsatisfactory 1 2 3 4 5 Satisfactory

2. I boldly respond to rumors, but I do not take revenge.

In a straightforward, sensitive, and nondefensive way, I deny the rumors to those who have stated them.
Unsatisfactory 1 2 3 4 5 Satisfactory

I interpret the situation to those who are close to me, who really know the truth, and who will be able to defend me to those who have been negatively influenced by the rumor.
Unsatisfactory 1 2 3 4 5 Satisfactory

I pray for personal strength emotionally and physically to handle the anxiety and stress caused by this experience.
Unsatisfactory 1 2 3 4 5 Satisfactory

I pray for those who have hurt me, whether maliciously or naively.
Unsatisfactory 1 2 3 4 5 Satisfactory

3. I do not allow fear to cloud my thinking so as to act irrationally and do something foolish.
Unsatisfactory 1 2 3 4 5 Satisfactory

Set a Goal

With God's help, I will begin immediately to carry out the following goal in my life:

_____

_____

_____

_____

Memorize the Following Scripture

> *But sanctify Christ as Lord in your hearts, always being ready to make a **defense** to everyone who asks you to give an account for the hope that is in you, yet with **gentleness and reverence**; and keep a good conscience so that in the thing in which you are **slandered**, those who revile your good behavior in Christ may be put to shame.*
> 1 Peter 3:15–16

Chapter 11

A Water Gate Experience

Read Nehemiah 8:1–9:38

Very few key leaders ever succeed in isolation. Moses had Aaron—and later Joshua. Joshua had Caleb; Elijah had Elisha; Peter had John; Paul had Barnabas—and later Silas.

Though it may appear that Nehemiah completed his task basically alone, it's not true. He would be the first to pay a great tribute to Ezra—the man who arrived in Jerusalem fourteen years before Nehemiah came on the scene. This old scribe had laid the "foundation" for Nehemiah's success—not in terms of bricks and stones, but in terms of the Law of God. Without this spiritual foundation, there would have been no wall!

Ezra was deeply committed to understanding and obeying God's will. More than that, he was committed to teaching others the will of God. This is very clear in the book that bears his name. "Ezra had set his heart to *study* the law of the Lord, and to *practice* it, and to *teach* His statutes and ordinances in Israel" (Ezra 7:10).

Ezra Did His Homework!

Ezra took his task seriously. He made sure that he did his own personal homework before he tried to communicate the laws of God to others.

A Diligent Student

Ezra devoted himself to learning the Word of God. He knew that before he could teach God's truth effectively to others, he had to understand it himself. Paul's exhortation to Timothy centuries later can certainly be applied to this Old Testament scribe. "Be diligent," Paul wrote, "to present yourself approved to God as a workman who does not need to be ashamed, handling accurately the word of truth" (2 Tim. 2:15).

A Faithful Practitioner

Ezra not only was a diligent student of God's laws, but he made sure he applied God's truth to his own life before he tried to get others to respond in obedience. He had "set his heart to *practice* it." He didn't ask people to do something he was not doing himself.

An Anointed Servant

Within the space of three verses, we discover another reason why Ezra had such a successful ministry. It wasn't simply his knowledge of Scripture nor even his ability to apply it. Rather, we read that "the hand of the Lord his God was upon him" (Ezra 7:6, 9).

God chose to bless Ezra in a special way. As always, there was a direct connection between his commitment to both knowing and doing the will of God and the way in which the Lord granted him favor among those in the pagan environment as well as those in Israel. There's no question, Ezra had a dynamic relationship with the God he loved and served.

A Deplorable Situation

The moral and spiritual condition of the people in Jerusalem was deplorable when Ezra first arrived. But as he prayerfully carried on his teaching ministry among the people, they gradually began to respond in obedience to the laws of God. By the time Nehemiah had arrived in Jerusalem, Ezra had laid an important foundation in Scripture. We now begin to understand why the people responded so readily when Nehemiah challenged them to "arise and build." True, it had to do with the fact that Nehemiah had put together a very careful plan. But more importantly, it had to do with the way in which Ezra had prepared these people to accept Nehemiah's challenge.

"I'm Ashamed and Embarrassed!"

There had been times—particularly when he first arrived in Jerusalem—when Ezra was so appalled at the immoral condition of the people that he had torn his garments and had pulled out some of the hair from his head and beard (see Ezra 9:3). Falling on his knees and with outstretched hands lifted to God, he had confessed the sins of the people: "O my God, I am ashamed and embarrassed to lift up my face to Thee, my God, for our iniquities have risen above our heads, and our guilt has grown even to the heavens" (v. 6).

A Breakthrough

How many days and weeks and perhaps months Ezra prayed and wept before God, we're not told. We do know that while he was "praying and making confession, weeping and prostrating himself before the house of God," a large group of people involving whole families gathered one day and joined him in his weeping and confession (10:1). This was a breakthrough—the beginning point of revival and renewal in Israel. If this hadn't happened, Nehemiah may not have been able to rally the people to tackle the rebuilding process.

A Miracle at the Water Gate

Once the wall was completed, "all the people gathered as one man at the square which was in front of the Water Gate, and they asked Ezra the scribe to bring the book of the law of Moses which the LORD had given to Israel (Neh. 8:1). You can imagine how much this request must have thrilled Ezra.

For days he had watched the people rebuild the walls against impossible odds. He had watched them respond with enthusiasm to Nehemiah's challenges. He had seen them lift their hearts in prayer to God when they sensed they could not succeed by themselves. How thrilled he must have been to see their motivation to trust God to help them accomplish what humanly speaking was an impossible task. But how much more excited he must have been when the people themselves—after the wall was rebuilt—gathered on their own in front of the Water Gate and asked him once again to read from the Law of God. All of his previous pain and agony must have faded away in view of their eagerness and openness to know more of the will of God.

When You're Discouraged, Remember Ezra

It's easy to get discouraged in ministry. More than we like to admit, one of the primary causes for this discouragement is the way some Christians respond—or should I say, *do not respond*—to our efforts.

When you're tempted to be discouraged, remember Ezra. Remember his weeks and months of prayer and weeping before God, confessing the sins of the people. Remember their slow response—that it took time both to teach and model obedience to the will of God. It took incredible patience and perseverance.

But also remember that the people eventually responded to the Word of God. Their hearts melted before the Lord. And be sure to remember that the day finally came—fourteen years later—when they, on their own, asked for Ezra to teach the Word of God. Perhaps we also need to ask ourselves questions in times of discouragement—"How much have I prayed and persevered for the people I minister to? How long have I been faithful?"

Ezra's Pulpit

What a sight it must have been! Ezra stood on a platform above the people behind the wooden podium that had been made especially for this occasion (see Neh. 8:4). On his right stood six men and on his left stood seven more. As he opened the Book of the Law, the people stood up to express their reverence for God's Word (see v. 5).

Then Ezra Prayed

Apparently lifting his hands toward heaven, Ezra "blessed the Lord the great God" (v. 6). At this moment, we're not given the specific content of his prayer. But it must have been similar to the prayer that is recorded in the next chapter: "O may Thy glorious name be blessed and exalted above all blessing and praise! Thou alone art the Lord. Thou hast made the heavens, the heaven of heavens with all their host, the earth and all that is on it, the seas and all that is in them. Thou dost give life to all of them and the heavenly host bows down before Thee" (9:5–6).

The people's response to Ezra's prayer must have been an ecstatic experience for this old priest and scribe. For years he had labored diligently to communicate God's truth to the people. And now as he looked out over this vast crowd of people, numbering in the thousands and gathered in the Water Gate square, he saw them lift their hands toward heaven as they shouted in response, "Amen, Amen!" Then they fell on their knees—evidently without being prompted—and bowed low with their faces to the ground as they "worshiped the Lord" (8:6).

A Great Communication Challenge

Nehemiah doesn't explain in detail exactly how Ezra read and explained God's law to this large crowd that may have numbered somewhere between thirty and fifty thousand people (see

7:66–67). However, we can use our imagination. Ezra must have read sections of the law in the presence of *all* the people (see 8:3). Then at certain points, all of the Levites must have circulated out among the people and interpreted and explained what Ezra had read as the people gathered in small groups—perhaps divided down by households (see vv. 7–8).

Remember, too, that Ezra read from the Hebrew Bible since many of the people were no longer fluent in their mother tongue. This was particularly true of the younger generation. Many of them had intermarried with various non-Jewish groups and learned another language. This is why Nehemiah records that Ezra and the Levites "read from the book, from the law of God, *translating to give the sense* so that they understood the reading" (v. 8). This was not simply an exercise in explaining what God's Word meant; rather, they had to translate from one language to another—and at the same time, make sure that the translation was accurate enough to convey the true meaning of the biblical text.

Positive Attitudes—Appropriate Actions

Not only did the children of Israel demonstrate their eagerness to revere and comprehend the Word of God, but they immediately responded with obedience. This is the true test of "hearing" and "understanding." They translated their positive attitudes into appropriate actions.

1. What they heard touched their emotions. When the searchlight of Scripture fell on their lifestyles, the children of Israel quickly discerned they had fallen far short of God's standard of righteousness. They literally wept before the Lord (see v. 9). They were overcome with godly sorrow.

2. Israel's sadness over their sins eventually turned to joy (see vv. 10–12). The more the children of Israel learned from the law of God, the more they understood how displeased God was with their sins. But they also began to understand His long-suffering,

His patience, and His willingness to forgive and restore them if they responded in obedience.

However, moving from sadness to joy took time. In fact, Nehemiah, Ezra, and the Levites had to actually encourage the people to stop mourning and weeping and to begin to rejoice and celebrate the Lord's forgiveness. Eventually, the people responded and "went away to eat, to drink, to send portions and to celebrate a great festival, *because they understood* the words which had been made known to them" (v. 12).

3. The leaders in Israel began to assume their God-ordained responsibilities for spiritual leadership. After Ezra had shared the Law of God with the total congregation, we read that a smaller group gathered around Ezra to learn even more of God's law (v. 13). This, of course, was a very important key in sustaining the renewal and revival that had begun in Israel. If this kind of work is to continue in the hearts of people, it must continue at the leadership level. Again, what made this even more encouraging to Ezra is that this was also a voluntary response. God's Spirit was definitely at work in the hearts of Israel's leaders.

We mustn't forget that Nehemiah's strong stand against social injustices that were taking place among the leaders no doubt helped set the stage for spiritual revival. In this sense, Ezra was continuing to build upon Nehemiah's efforts—just as Nehemiah had built upon Ezra's initial work in teaching the laws of God.

4. The people celebrated the Feast of Tabernacles (see vv. 14–18). As the leaders in Israel learned more and more of God's will for their lives, they discovered that the Lord had designed a special experience for all of them that was to take place during the Feast of Tabernacles. They were to live in temporary shelters for seven days (see Lev. 23:33–44; Deut. 16:13–15). This may seem strange to us, but God's rationale for this experience was profound. The children of Israel had wandered in the wilderness for years living in temporary dwellings. On the one hand, this wilderness experience was extended because of Israel's unwillingness to obey God and enter the land. On the other hand, all during this time, God protected them and provided for their needs. He never forsook them.

God never wanted His people to forget this experience. That's why He established the Feast of Tabernacles. Once the leaders in Israel rediscovered this special ritual, they reinstated it in Israel. Whole families built booths and lived in them for seven days. You can imagine the questions that were asked by the children and youth—and the unique opportunity this afforded their parents to communicate their sacred history (see Lev. 23:43).

5. *The children of Israel separated themselves from pagan alliances and practices (see Neh. 10:28–30).* Separation of course did not mean *isolation,* for they could not remove themselves from their surroundings and the environment. However, the people determined to separate themselves from activities and involvements with unbelieving people that were in direct violation of the law of God, particularly intermarriage and idolatrous and immoral behavior.

Becoming God's Man Today

Principles to Live By

As we apply this study to our lives, let's focus on the divine principles that relate to the Word of God. After all, it was the Scriptures that were foundational in bringing renewal to Israel. Without this foundation that Ezra laid, Nehemiah could not possibly have succeeded in rebuilding the walls in fifty-two days. Furthermore, he would have had a terrible time dealing with the social injustices in Israel.

Principle 1. We must read the Bible, understand it, and apply it to our lives!

We're indeed fortunate. Not only do we have access to the Old Testament, but we have at our disposal God's complete written revelation. Furthermore, in recent years modern translations have multiplied, causing the Scriptures to come alive with meaning. We're no longer locked into Old English, needing someone to "translate" and interpret the archaic words.

We Have Bibles Galore

Think for a moment about what has happened in the last fifty years. God has raised up hundreds of modern-day "Levites"—men and women who thoroughly know Old Testament Hebrew and New Testament Greek, and in turn have given us many different translations of the Bible that are both literal and contemporary. We can walk into thousands of bookstores everywhere and buy a variety of Bibles that have been translated into modern English.

Principle 2. We must determine to devote ourselves to a serious study of the Bible.

Many of us do not study the Bible regularly on our own—partly because we simply neglect this unique opportunity and responsibility. Most of us, however, don't know *how* to study the Bible. We have no method. We get discouraged and simply give up.

Preliminary Steps

1. Determine that you are going to study the Bible regularly.
2. Decide on a study time that fits best into your own personal schedule.
3. Choose the place that's best for you.
4. Select a good literal, but modern translation of the Bible (I suggest the New International Version or the New American Standard Bible, although I also enjoy using the New King James Version).
5. Use a study guide that:
   ➤ is simple enough to be practical for you;
   ➤ is flexible enough to fit into your schedule;

➤ helps you read, interpret, and apply the Scriptures.

6. Purchase a notebook so you can record the results of your study.

7. Select and purchase a quality hymnbook you can use for meditation, worship, and praise.

Principle 3. We must learn how to study the Bible.

The forms on the following two pages provide a simple plan for personal Bible study.[1] The first is a sample to demonstrate its use, the second is for you to duplicate and use in your own study. There are spaces to record the passage, a title for your study (which you'll want to determine after you've completed your study), and a date. In addition, there are eight simple steps for effective Bible study.

Here's How!

Step 1—Pray. Praise God and ask the Holy Spirit to illumine your mind. Praising and thanking God for who He is and what He has done is a good way to prepare your heart for personal Bible study. You might try reading the words of both the old hymns of the faith as well as contemporary songs. For example, "Great Is Thy Faithfulness" or "How Great Thou Art" are excellent illustrations of hymns that focus on God's character.

NOTE: You might try singing some of the hymns (if you're alone). Don't worry what you sound like. Simply make a joyful sound to the Lord even if you have difficulty "making music." I guarantee that God will enjoy it!

Step 2—Survey. Read the passage quickly. It's important to get an overview of the passage of Scripture before studying it in detail. As just stated, go over the passage *quickly*. Don't get bogged down with details. Try to look at the "forest" first. Your next step will be to go back and look at the "individual trees."

Step 3—Read. Read the passage carefully. Note that steps 3 and 4 should be done at the same time.

Personal Bible Study Guide

Passage: *Philippians 1:1–6*   Title: _____   Date: _____

1. Pray...   5. Interpret...
2. Survey...   6. Apply...
3. Read...   7. Pray...
4. Observe...   8. Share...

Section 1 – Reading and Recording
What does the Bible say? Copy key statements and verses from the passage.

"I thank my God . . . remembrance of you." v. 3

"I am confident . . . He . . . will perfect it." v. 6

Section 2 – Interpreting and Understanding
What do these statements mean? Put in your own words (outling, ask questions, etc.)

He had pleasant memories of them. Why? See Acts 16 for clues.

He prayed for them regularly.

Section 3 – Applying and Obeying
How do these statements apply to my life? What will I do?

What Christians do I remember this way and pray for?
Here are some for today:
   Bruce Wilkinson
   Renee Getz
   Don Logue

When will I do it? _____*Immediately*_____
With whom will I do it? _____*Alone this morning, with my wife this evening*_____

Personal Bible Study Guide

Passage: _____ Title: _____ Date: _____

1. Pray…   5. Interpret…
2. Survey…   6. Apply…
3. Read…   7. Pray…
4. Observe…   8. Share…

Section 1 – Reading and Recording
What does the Bible say? Copy key statements and verses from the passage.

Section 2 – Interpreting and Understanding
What do these statements mean? Put in your own words (outling, ask questions, etc.)

Section 3 – Applying and Obeying
How do these statements apply to my life? What will I do?

When will I do it? _____

With whom will I do it? _____

Step 4—Observe. Look for biblical statements that are especially meaningful. Copy these statements in Section 1. As just
stated, steps 3 and 4 should be taken together. As you read
carefully, look for those statements that are particularly meaningful to you. The time you have for personal study and also the
nature of the passage will determine how many statements you
record in this section entitled "Reading and Recording." You
may actually decide to copy only one significant statement.

Step 5—Interpret. Record in section 2 what these biblical
statements mean. Interpreting the Scriptures is a very important
part of Bible study. Remember at this point you are not concen-
trating on application but, rather, on what the Bible is actually
teaching you in a literal, historical setting. You may outline what
it means and/or you may actually ask questions about what it
means. Don't be concerned if you don't understand everything
you have observed and written down.

NOTE: In interpreting the Scriptures, be sure to consider
the larger context of the passage you're studying.

Step 6—Apply. Record in section 3 what you can do to apply
these biblical statements in your own life. Application may at
times be the most difficult phase in personal Bible study. It's very
easy and convenient to stop with the process of *observing* and
interpreting. But, to really benefit from your study, you must
think about how the biblical statements you have copied on your
sheet apply to your life personally. It will help you to answer the
question "what will I do?" as a result of this study. It will also
help you to answer the questions, "When will I do it?" and
"With whom will I do it?"

NOTE: It's not always possible to answer these questions in
great detail. In some instances, when you answer the question
"With whom will I do it?" you may simply respond that it will
involve your relationship with God.

Remember also that sometimes applications are cumulative.
If you are studying related passages over several days, you may
discover that you will be led to a culminating application as a

result of several days of study. In other words, don't be frustrated if you have difficulty applying every single statement.

Step 7—Pray. Use your observations and applications as a basis for prayer and praise. If you're like I am, you may have difficulty talking to God in a meaningful way—particularly in private. Your personal Bible studies will help you to have something to say to the Lord on a regular basis. Your three sections will provide you with a prayer outline. Use what you have written as a basis for your communication with the Lord. When you come to Section 3, you can ask God specifically to help you to apply to your own life what the Holy Spirit has taught you.

Step 8—Share. Look for a natural opportunity to encourage someone with what you've learned. This is not always possible. The important word here is *natural.* If you ask God to provide you with these opportunities, you'll be surprised at how they appear in the daily routines of life. And when they're "natural," you will not feel as if you are demonstrating a "super-spiritual" attitude that could be misinterpreted.

Becoming a Man of the Word

As you evaluate the following principles, pray and ask the Holy Spirit to impress on your heart at least one lesson in the area of Bible study you need to apply more effectively in your own life. Then write out a specific goal. For example, you may discover that you have simply been reading the Scriptures rather than making good observations and applications. Or, perhaps you have neglected to pray before and after you study.

➤ We must read the Bible, understand it, and apply it to our lives!

➤ We must determine to devote ourselves to a serious study of the Bible.

➤ We must learn how to study the Bible!

Set a Goal

With God's help, I will begin immediately to carry out the following goal in my life:

_____

_____

_____

_____

Memorize the Following Scripture

Be diligent to present yourself approved to God as a workman who does not need to be ashamed, handling accurately the word of truth.
2 TIMOTHY 2:15

Chapter 12

A Leader's Toughest Task
Read Nehemiah 13:4–31

I wish we could conclude Nehemiah's story with a beautiful and happy ending. Wouldn't it be exhilarating and encouraging to discover that the children of Israel continued to serve God faithfully for years to come—even after Nehemiah left Jerusalem to return to Susa to serve King Artaxerxes. Unfortunately, it didn't turn out that way! Within a relatively short period of time, the children of Israel returned to their old ways of doing things—violating God's laws and allowing the world's system to press them into its mold.

Tobiah, who had caused Nehemiah untold trouble, had set up housekeeping in "the courts of the house of God" (13:7). The people had stopped paying their tithes, making it impossible for the Levites to function as spiritual leaders in Israel (see v. 10).

They were also violating the Sabbath, using this day as an opportunity to buy and sell throughout Jerusalem (see v. 15). They even invited their pagan neighbors to "set up shop" and sell their wares (see v. 16).

The most tragic departure from God's will involved inter-marriage with their pagan neighbors. They had allowed their sons to "marry women from Ashdod, Ammon, and Moab" (v. 23).

How Could This Happen?

I'm sure Nehemiah was scratching his head and asking this same question. After all, as God's people, they had experienced social renewal when Nehemiah dealt with the injustices against the poor. They had experienced spiritual renewal because of Ezra's teaching.

They had publicly committed to "keep and to observe all the commandments of God" (10:29). A number of their leaders had even signed a sealed document committing themselves to obey the Lord and keep His laws (see 9:38–10:27). And once the wall was totally complete, they dedicated it to the Lord with a great service of worship and praise (see 12:27–47).

Initially No Regrets

I'm sure when Nehemiah eventually left Jerusalem to return to his duties as cupbearer to King Artaxerxes, his heart was filled with joy—not so much because of his own accomplishments as a leader, but because of what had happened to his people. He had great hopes for Israel with no regrets regarding the twelve years he'd spent in Jerusalem serving as governor. I'm confident he felt that all he had personally suffered and sacrificed was worth it in view of Israel's response and accomplishments. God had answered his prayers and honored his faithfulness again and again.

But Now, Keen Disappointment

Imagine—if you can—Nehemiah's emotional responses when he returned to Jerusalem a relatively short time later (perhaps two years) to discover these startling changes had taken place among the children of Israel. How could his people be violating so many aspects of the covenant they had prepared and publicly signed. In some respects, this was a much more difficult experience for Nehemiah than when he first arrived in Jerusalem years before

"Not Tobiah!"

Nehemiah was horrified to find that Eliashib—the *high priest* in Israel—had prepared a special guest room for Tobiah in the temple. This was one of the serious consequences of intermarriage (see 13:4).

Tobiah was one of his archenemies. He had joined Sanballat and Geshem to try to stop him from rebuilding the wall. During that time, Tobiah had been involved in a conspiracy to attack the children of Israel. He'd also been part of a diabolical scheme to harm Nehemiah—perhaps even to assassinate him. When all of these efforts failed, he continued to do everything else he could to discredit Nehemiah—including writing intimidating letters filled with lies (see 6:19).

What made all of this even more shocking to Nehemiah is that the large chamber that the high priest had prepared for Tobiah included several rooms where the tithes and offerings of the people were stored so that the priestly ministry could continue in Israel as God had outlined in His law. These were also the rooms where the utensils and frankincense were stored, which the priest used in offering sacrifices to the Lord.

Euphemistically speaking, Nehemiah was upset. He couldn't believe his eyes. Nehemiah became so angry—and understandably so—that he went into the temple and literally "threw all of Tobiah's household goods" out the door (13:8). He then "gave an order" for the rooms to be cleansed (v. 9). Nehemiah wanted every trace of Tobiah's presence removed from the temple. To put it bluntly, he had the room disinfected!

When Nehemiah investigated to find out why all of this had happened, he discovered that the children of Israel had failed in their commitment to pay their tithes and offerings. The rooms Tobiah occupied—which were to be the "storehouse" for the gifts of the people—were empty. Furthermore, the Levites and the others who were to live off of these offerings as they performed spiritual services for the people had to go back to their regular jobs (see v. 10).

A Critical and Heartbreaking Situation

Personally, I would have been tempted to turn around and head back to Susa. It would be easy to conclude that there was no hope for these people. I certainly would have felt greatly unappreciated for all that I had personally sacrificed to help them get restored and settled in Jerusalem and the surrounding area.

But not Nehemiah! He wasted no time in correcting this abuse. He called a meeting of all of the officials in Israel and reprimanded them for neglecting to make sure the children of Israel obeyed the Lord. Can you imagine their embarrassment when Nehemiah called to their attention in no uncertain terms that they had previously signed a document, promising before the Lord and the people that they would never again let this happen in Israel (see 10:32–39).

Nehemiah's next move was to call a meeting of all of the Levites; he "restored them to their posts" (13:11). Imagine all the consternation this created among the people. Some were probably rejoicing—while others were as mad as hornets! Probably the majority simply watched from the sidelines to see what was going to happen.

Knowing people's natural bent to be selfish, Nehemiah's greatest task was to convince the people to bring their tithes of grain, wine, and oil to the temple in order to meet the needs of their spiritual leaders. We're not told how he accomplished all this, but we know that he got the job done (see v. 12). It had to be emotionally and physically draining!

Profaning the Sabbath Day

Israel had also put in writing that they would not violate God's laws regarding the Sabbath day (see 10:31). However, they had broken this promise as well (13:15–22). Some "were treading wine presses on the sabbath, and bringing in sacks of grain and loading them on donkeys, as well as wine, grapes, figs, and all kinds of loads, and they brought them into Jerusalem on the sabbath day" (v. 15).

In addition, there were men of Tyre who actually moved into Jerusalem and set up their own businesses. The leaders in Israel allowed them to operate their shops seven days a week (v. 16)!

Nehemiah tackled this problem next. He "reprimanded the nobles of Judah and said to them, 'what is this evil thing you are doing, by profaning the sabbath day?'"(v. 17).

He confronted them with an even more penetrating question: "Did not your fathers do the same so that our God brought on us, and on this city, all this trouble? Yet you are adding to the wrath on Israel by profaning the sabbath" (v. 18).

How quickly God's people can regress when their spiritual leaders fail them. Evidently, as soon as Nehemiah had left for Susa, men like Tobiah quickly emerged and wielded their evil influence. It's possible that Nehemiah was caught off guard, not realizing how powerful, corrupt, and unrepentant these men actually were. After all, you'd think that twelve years would have been time enough to test their motives.

Violating Marriage Commitments

Once Nehemiah cleansed the temple, reestablished God's plan for the priesthood, and restored the Sabbath, he then faced his most difficult challenge (13:23–31). The children of Israel had also promised in writing that they would not intermarry with pagan people—those who did not worship and serve the one true God (see 10:30). Yet Nehemiah discovered they had flagrantly violated this commitment (see 13:23).

Nehemiah's Unprecedented Anger

Clearly, this frustrated Nehemiah more than the other sins! He was so angry with those who had committed this sin that he "contended with them and cursed them"—that is, he pronounced God's judgment upon them. The depth of his disappointment and the intensity of his anger is seen in that he "struck some of them and pulled out their hair, and made them swear by God, 'You shall not give your daughters to their sons, nor take of their daughters for your sons or for yourselves'" (v. 25).

What made this crisis so difficult to deal with is that it involved family relationships. It's difficult to imagine the anxiety, fear, anger, and frustration Nehemiah faced—and caused—when he confronted this problem so directly. But Nehemiah had no choice if he wanted to be a faithful spiritual leader. Furthermore, he knew by experience what had happened before when this sin was not dealt with in Israel.

This Caused Solomon's Downfall

This may seem like violent and inappropriate behavior for a man of God. However, when we interpret Nehemiah's actions against the backdrop of Israel's history, it's easier to understand his intense feelings.

This very sin was the primary reason why they were taken into Babylonian captivity in the first place. And this is why he reminded them of an important historical fact as he unleashed his righteous fury: "Did not Solomon king of Israel sin regarding these things? Yet among the many nations there was no king like him, and he was loved by his God, and God made him king over all Israel; nevertheless the foreign woman caused even him to sin" (v. 26).

Speaking from Experience

Nehemiah had personally experienced the results of Solomon's sin. This is why his parents had been carried off into captivity by the Babylonians. That's why he was a servant to King Artaxerxes. Nehemiah was deeply concerned that God's judgment might fall on Israel again. He knew the Lord would never tolerate this sin. If He had not allowed it in Solomon's life and had judged all Israel because of it, Nehemiah knew God would not allow it now.

Nehemiah's disappointment and anger at this moment was not nearly so much related to his feelings of being betrayed and taken for granted. Rather, he was more concerned about what this would mean to others in Israel who were attempting to obey God's laws.

Becoming God's Man Today

Principles to Live By

The final chapter in Nehemiah's life story leaves us with two important perspectives on leadership. The first involves the appointment of qualified leaders, and the second involves dealing with sin in the lives of God's people.

Principle 1. It's important to turn over the reins of leadership to spiritually qualified people.

One spiritually unqualified leader can destroy years of work in a very short period of time. It simply takes *one man with power to make decisions* to lead a multitude of people in the wrong direction. All he has to do is build around him a smaller group of like-minded people that share his own selfish and carnal agendas.

Nehemiah should know. It happened to him. He describes this awesome reality in the final chapter of his personal journal. Eliashib, the high priest in Israel, was definitely ill-equipped spiritually to perform his duties. If he had been "a man of God," he certainly wouldn't have allowed Tobiah to live in "the courts of the house of God" (13:7).

Family Politics

It's not possible to know all the reasons why this happened. We do know that "family politics" were certainly involved since Nehemiah recorded very specifically that Eliashib was "related to Tobiah"—obviously by marriage, since Tobiah was not a Jew (v. 4).

There were other factors as well. Because of his "family connections," Tobiah had ingratiated himself with a number of other key leaders in Israel, even while Nehemiah was still serving as governor. In fact, there were alliances established before the wall was ever completed. When Sanballat, Geshem, and Tobiah had made their final attempt to harm Nehemiah in order to keep him from completing the wall, we have a very specific statement regarding these alliances: "Also in those days many letters went from the nobles of Judah to Tobiah, and Tobiah's letters came to them. For many in Judah *were bound by oath to him* because he was the son-in-law of Shecaniah the son of Arah, and his son Jehohanan had married the daughter of Meshullam the son of Berechiah" (6:17–18).

Unanswered Questions

All of these family connections gave Tobiah an inside track among key leaders in Israel. But this raises several questions. With this knowledge, why did Nehemiah leave Jerusalem knowing about these alliances? Had these men managed to deceive him for nearly twelve years, giving the impression that they were sincerely committed to practicing God's laws, but at the same time, waiting to make their move once Nehemiah left? Or, was this simply a mistake on Nehemiah's part?

It's difficult to answer these questions. Frankly, I hesitate to fault Nehemiah. Being a leader myself, I know how easy it is for circumstances and events to get beyond our control. Try as we might, we can't foresee all future problems and make decisions that will guarantee positive results for years to come.

On the other hand, I also know that it is possible for the greatest leaders in the world to have "blind spots" and make decisions that they wish they'd never made. It's certainly possible that this happened to Nehemiah. He could have made some bad judgments. Perhaps things were going so well in Judah—in Jerusalem particularly—that he failed to pray for God's wisdom in some of these decisions. Perhaps he simply began to rely on his own wisdom and abilities. That's every spiritual leader's tendency—and certainly, it could have happened to Nehemiah.

Great Strengths Can Be Great Weaknesses

As I reflect on my own experience as a leader—particularly as a church planting pastor—I now realize as never before how important it is to select key leaders carefully. The wrong man in a strategic position can destroy a ministry almost "overnight." I've seen that happen.

In fact, early on, when we were starting a number of branch churches out of our home-based church, one of my fellow elders said to me one day, "Gene, your greatest strength is to trust people. Your greatest weakness is to trust people you shouldn't trust!"

My friend made that statement after I had made some unfortunate decisions in recommending certain leaders to serve as pastors of these various churches. Time demonstrated that some of these men were not as qualified as they should have been—even though I believed they were. Since that time, I've tried to be much more discriminate, to seek more counsel from others in making leadership appointments, and to develop better systems for screening potential leaders. The most important thing I've learned is to seek God's will more faithfully in making these appointments.

Developing Balance

After almost forty years in the ministry, I can look back and see that most problems that evolved in various ministry situations happened because of ill-equipped and unqualified leaders. I'm simply verifying the principle we can learn from Nehemiah's experience when he turned the reins of leadership over to others when he left Jerusalem. Unfortunately, some of the key men he trusted betrayed that trust. We can never be too careful.

On the other hand, we must not refuse to delegate because we're afraid to trust people. We simply need to develop a healthy balance based on doing all we can to apply biblical principles in selecting leaders and, at the same time, realizing that even the most trustworthy leaders can fail—including ourselves. This may be what happened in Nehemiah's situation.

Principle 2. One of our God-given responsibilities as leaders is to teach people God's will, and when people violate His will, we're to confront that disobedience with biblical truth.

Church discipline and how to carry it out is a large subject in itself. We don't have space to do it justice in this chapter. Rather, I've chosen to concentrate on the three areas of disobedience Nehemiah had to confront and how these sins and failures should be dealt with in the lives of Christians today.

1. Dishonoring God in Our Associations with Unbelievers

We see this principle violated when Eliashib allowed Tobiah to live in the temple area. It was even more dramatically violated when the children of Israel encouraged marriages with people who did not believe in the one true God.

This important principle is reiterated by Paul in the New Testament in his second letter to the Corinthians. His instructions are specific and to the point:

> Do not be bound together with unbelievers; for what partnership have righteousness and lawlessness, or what fellowship has light with darkness? Or what harmony has Christ with Belial, or what has a believer in common with an unbeliever? Or what agreement has the temple of God with idols? For we are the temple of the living God. (2 Cor. 6:14–16)

Paul clearly tied this New Testament teaching to what we've seen happen in Israel by quoting a series of Old Testament passages:

For we are the temple of the living God; just as God said, "I will dwell in them and walk among them; and I will be their God, and they shall be My people. Therefore, come out from their midst and be separate," says the Lord. "And do not touch what is unclean; and I will welcome you. And I will be a father to you, and you shall be sons and daughters to Me," says the Lord Almighty. (2 Cor. 6:16–18)

What This Doesn't Mean. Paul was not teaching that we must separate totally from non-Christians. Separation does not mean isolation. Paul also dealt with this very practical issue in his first letter to the Corinthians. Earlier, he had instructed these New Testament believers "not to associate with immoral people"— meaning a "so-called brother if he should be an immoral person, or covetous, or an idolater, or a reviler, or a drunkard, or a swindler" (1 Cor. 5:9, 11).

Some of the Corinthians misunderstood Paul and thought he was saying they should not associate at all with non-Christians who are living this kind of lifestyle. Paul quickly clarified what he meant: "I did not at all mean with the immoral people of this world, or with the covetous and swindlers, or with idolaters; for then you would have to go out of the world" (1 Cor. 5:10).

It's impossible to live in this world without associating with non-Christians. In fact, if we break all ties, how can we carry out the Great Commission to lead people to Jesus Christ? In fact, some of our greatest witnessing opportunities come when we're working side by side with unbelievers.

What This Does Mean. Paul was teaching all of us as Christians that in our associations with non-Christians, we must be a witness of Christ's life and His message of salvation. But we must not develop relationships that will influence us negatively and cause us to participate in their sins.

Intermarriage. The most powerful lesson we can learn from what happened in Israel as well as from the New Testament setting in Corinth is if we marry people who do not share our salvation experience, we're walking into serious trouble. We are violating God's perfect will—and when we do, that always creates difficulties in our lives.

It's true that in some instances it works out. Sometimes the unsaved partner becomes a Christian. In other instances, the person may not be a Christian but is tolerant of the other partner's faith in Christ. In some rare instances, the non-Christian partner may even support the spouse's spiritual commitments. However, in most instances, a marriage between a Christian and a non-Christian leads to disappointment, heartbreak, and often separation and divorce.

Please don't misunderstand. I'm not advocating that once we've made this decision that we should try to undo it. Two wrongs don't make a right. The important point is that we forewarn Christians so that they don't make this mistake—because once they've made it, they'll have to do everything they can to make it work.

Business Associations. Another area of application is in our business relationships. If I'm an employee, I can resign. But if I'm a partner, it's an association that is far more complex. In that sense, it's very similar to marriage. If we're not careful, we'll be compromising our Christian convictions in order to survive in a contractual relationship.

I know a Christian businessman who went into partnership with a non-Christian whose value system was out of harmony with Christian principles. It was an equal partnership. This kind of "marriage" was devastating and a "divorce" was inevitable, creating a great deal of heartache and emotional pain for everyone involved.

2. Dishonoring God with Our Material Possessions

God established certain laws in Israel regarding tithing. His people were to give one-tenth of all of their material possessions to meet the physical needs of the Levites. Under Ezra's teaching, they once again became obedient to the Lord. But when Nehemiah returned from Susa, they had stopped tithing. Consequently, the Levites were not able to minister to the people spiritually, which caused even more moral and spiritual deterioration in Israel.

Generosity under Grace. "Tithing" per se is not reiterated in the New Testament. In fact, it's true that Israel set aside more than 10 percent for the Lord's work. They were also to set aside 10 percent for a special celebration in Jerusalem (see Deut. 12:5–6, 11, 18). Furthermore, *every third year* an additional 10 percent was collected to care for strangers, the fatherless, widows, and any additional needs the Levites might have (see Deut. 14:28–29). In other words, the children of Israel were to give approximately 23 percent of their resources each year to carry on the work of God.

In the New Testament, God introduces us to guidelines for giving that rise above the law. Paul outlines these principles in his Corinthian letters.

1. We are to give systematically. When writing to the Corinthians, Paul instructed them to set aside a sum of money "upon the first day of the week . . . as God hath prospered them" (1 Cor. 16:2, KJV). Obviously, there are cultural factors involved in this "pattern," but the principle is clear. Though we may be paid every two weeks, or monthly, or even in some instances yearly, we are to set aside a certain amount regularly to give to God's work. This means our giving should be planned just as carefully as any other item in our budgets. And God's work should be first.

2. We are to give proportionately. In the same verse, Paul instructed the Corinthians that each person should give "in keeping with his income" (NIV). If we make a lot of money, we should give a lot of money. If we don't make as much money, we are to give less. But everyone is to give—no matter how small or large the income.

3. We are to give cheerfully. In Paul's second Letter to the Corinthians, he laid down a third guideline: "Remember this: Whoever sows sparingly will also reap sparingly, and whoever sows generously will also reap generously. Each man should give what he has decided in his heart to give, not reluctantly or under compulsion, for God loves a *cheerful* giver" (2 Cor. 9:6–7, NIV).

God is not pleased if we give reluctantly and under compulsion. This is the principle of grace. Freely we have received and freely we are to give. This is true worship. This demonstrates true gratitude to God for what He has given to us in Jesus Christ.

4. We can expect God to meet our needs. After Paul instructed the Corinthians to give regularly, generously, and cheerfully, he also wrote, "God is able to make all grace abound to you, so that in all things at all times, having all that you need, you will abound in every good work" (2 Cor. 9:8, NIV).

With this promise, God has not guaranteed us that He will multiply our income. However, He has promised to meet our needs. And furthermore, I know of very few instances where people have given generously that God has not poured out unusual blessings on them—both spiritually and financially.

126 Biblical Principles. As Christian leaders, we are responsible to teach people these principles of giving. In fact, the elders in my church charged me with the responsibility to teach our own people their stewardship responsibilities. I countered by inviting them to study the Bible to see exactly what God taught on the subject of material possessions. It was an exciting process for all of us. As a result, we discovered *126 biblical principles* to guide Christians in the use of their material possessions. In this chapter, I've only shared four of those principles. It may surprise you to discover that the Bible says more about the subject of how Christians are to use their material possessions than any other subject other than God Himself.[1]

Christians have been influenced by materialism—which is one reason why they do not give as they should. Some studies reveal that Christians give an average of only 2 percent of their income. When you subtract those who faithfully give 10 percent or more, you can only come up with the conclusion that a lot of Christians are giving next to nothing—and you're right!

Though materialism has taken its toll, one of the reasons Christians don't give as they should is that they have not been taught their responsibility. Another reason Christians continue to disobey God is that they are not confronted with their disobedience. As Christian leaders, we cannot hide our heads in the sand and ignore this important responsibility. Nehemiah's example certainly teaches us this lesson.

If Israel under law was to give 10 percent so the Levites could carry out the work of God, this should at least be a *starting point* for Christians who are living under grace. I'm always encouraged when I read the stories of Christians who have struggled with the concept of tithing (giving at least 10 percent) and then have made that decision—not out of obligation, but out of love for Christ. The end result is always exciting.

Mary Crowley's Story. I've always been impressed by Mary Crowley's experience. She spent her early years as an orphan. In her quest for security and hope, she made a bad decision in marriage and it ended in divorce. She was left with two children and full responsibility for their welfare during the Depression.

Mary's income was so small that she could hardly pay her bills. "There was just no way that I could tithe," she concluded. As she sat at her kitchen table after the children were asleep one evening, she figured up her stack of bills, her budget for groceries, her rent, her housekeeping expenses, her bus fare for going to work and church. "If I added 10 percent of my salary to the debit side of my budget," she thought, "there would be nothing at all left in the miscellaneous column—no money for Christmas presents, books for the kids, or the dentist."[2]

But the more Mary prayed, the more she was impressed that she should set aside 10 percent of her income for her church—not out of obligation but because she wanted to honor God. The story that unfolded in her life is incredible.

Mary is now in heaven, but while she lived on earth, the Lord enabled her to build a multimillion-dollar enterprise called Home Interiors and Gifts, Inc. The annual sales have reached millions of dollars. And each year she gave multiplied thousands of those dollars to God's work. She became one of the most benevolent Christians I've ever known.

Will God do this for every Christian who is faithful in giving? Not at all! The facts are that Mary Crowley developed this business because of a lot of hard work, intense motivation, and prayer. But intricately blended with that work and prayer is the fact that she was faithful to the Lord with her money. And the more He blessed her, the more she gave. She became a "proportionate giver." I'm convinced that God does honor the application of this principle in our lives.

3. Dishonoring God with Our Time

In the Old Testament, God established the Sabbath as a day of rest for Israel. It was a rigid law and was not to be violated in any way. In the New Testament, God does not place us under this strict system. Rather, every day is to be a special day for God.

But just as Christians take advantage of God's grace once they have been released from a strict law of giving, we also take advantage of God's grace once released from a strict Sabbath law. How easy it is to neglect our time spent in service for God, with other Christians, and with our families. The author of the Letter to the Hebrews speaks to this issue pointedly: "Let us consider how to stimulate one another to love and good deeds, not forsaking our own assembling together, as is the habit of some, but encouraging one another; and all the more, as you see the day drawing near" (Heb. 10:24–25).

Becoming a Responsible Leader

As you evaluate the following principles and questions, pray and ask the Holy Spirit to impress on your heart one lesson you need to apply more effectively in your life as a leader—in your home, in your church, or in your business life. Then write out a specific goal. For example, you may recognize that you are not cautious enough when you appoint leaders to handle significant areas of responsibility.

> It's very important to turn over the reins of leadership to spiritually qualified people.

> One of our God-given responsibilities as leaders is to teach people God's will, and when people violate His will, we're to confront that disobedience with biblical truth.

1. As a Christian leader, how careful am I when I appoint other leaders? Do I realize that one person who is ill-equipped spiritually can literally destroy what it has taken years to build? Do I have a system for evaluating leaders?[3]

2. Am I honoring God in my associations with other people? Am I allowing non-Christians to drag me down spiritually by causing me to do things that are out of the will of God?

3. Do I honor God with my material possessions? What percentage of my income am I giving to God? Am I giving proportionately as God has blessed me? Am I faithful in meeting the physical needs of those who minister to me? Have I ever committed to give a minimum of 10 percent to the Lord's work?

4. Do I honor God with my time? How do I spend the Lord's day? Am I negligent in spending time encouraging and building up other Christians? What about my own personal program for rest and relaxation? Am I honoring God with my total being—body, mind, and soul?

5. As a Christian leader, am I both teaching people these important biblical principles as well as exhorting them in proper fashion when they violate these principles?

6. Am I following Nehemiah's example as a leader by not asking people to do things I'm not doing myself?

Set a Goal

With God's help, I will begin immediately to carry out the following goal in my life:

_____

_____

_____

_____

Memorize the Following Scripture

And He gave some as apostles, and some as prophets, and some as evangelists, and some as pastors and teachers, for the equipping of the saints for the work of service, to the building up of the body of Christ; until we all attain to the unity of the faith, and of the knowledge of the Son of God, to a mature man, to the measure of the stature which belongs to the fulness of Christ.
EPHESIANS 4:11–13

Notes

Chapter 2

1. There is a difference of opinion regarding this historical theory. Some Bible interpreters believe that the term Artaxerxes was a general title which applied to more than one ruler and in this instance, the "Artaxerxes" Nehemiah served as cupbearer was a different man than the one Ezra referred to in chapter 4 of the book that bears his name. However, others believe that Ezra 4:6–23 is a parenthetical passage and refers to the same Artaxerxes as mentioned in Nehemiah.

After carefully considering both views, I have personally accepted the latter view as the most feasible. You will note that I have followed this historical hypothesis in explaining the text of Nehemiah.

Chapter 4

1. Cyril Barber, Nehemiah and the Dynamics of Effective Leadership (Neptune, N.J.: Loizeaux Brothers, 1976), 49.
2. Ibid., 49.

Chapter 5

1. Lloyd Cory, *Quotable Quotations* (Wheaton, Ill.: Victor Books, 1985), 210.

2. Ibid., 211.

3. For an in-depth study of Elijah—and particularly how God dealt with his depression—see Gene A. Getz, *Elijah: Remaining Steadfast Through Uncertainty* (Nashville: Broadman & Holman, 1995).

Chapter 7

1. The actual meaning of chapter 4, verse 23 is vague in the Hebrew text. C. F. Keil translates, "And each laid his weapon on the right, viz. When he laid himself down at night to rest in his clothes, to be ready for fighting at the first signal from the watch." (Biblical Commentary on the Old Testament, the Books of Ezra, Nehemiah, Esther, [Grand Rapids: William B. Eerdmans Publishing Co., n.d.], 207). Though variously translated, the main point is clear both textually and contextually. They were ready to fight day and night.

2. Charles R. Swindoll, *Hand Me Another Brick* (Nashville: Thomas Nelson, Inc., 1978), 137.

3. John H. Yates, "Faith Is the Victory." Public domain.

4. F. Kefa Sempangi, *A Distant Grief* (Ventura, Calif.: Regal Books, 1979), 179–80.

Chapter 9

1. John Bartlett, *Familiar Quotations* (Boston: Little, Brown and Company, 1955), 475.

2. Charles Swindoll, *Hand Me Another Brick* (Nashville: Thomas Nelson, Inc., 1978), 113.

Chapter 10

1. Charles W. Colson, *Life Sentence* (Lincoln, Va.: Chosen Books, 1979), 51–52.

2. We're not sure of the exact location of the meeting place suggested by Sanballat and Geshem. C. F. Keil believes it was probably northwest of Jerusalem, not far from Bethel.

3. Colson, 51–52.

Chapter 11

1. Adapted from a Bible Study Guide developed by Chuck Miller of BARNABAS, Inc., an organization that specializes in Discipling Ministries Seminars, Box 218, Highland, California 92346. Used by permission.

Chapter 12

1. To pursue this subject further, see the following books: Gene A. Getz, *Biblical Theology of Material Possessions* (Chicago: Moody Press, 1990) and *Real Prosperity* (Chicago: Moody Press, 1990).

2. Mary C. Crowley, *Think Mink* (Old Tappan, N.J.: Fleming H. Revell Company, 1976), 33.

3. For a careful study on the qualities for leadership, see Gene A. Getz, *Measure of a Man* (Ventura, Calif.: Regal Books, 1974).